ON A COUNTRY ROAD

25 Bicycle Rides in Beautiful and Historic
Southeastern Pennsylvania

Barry and Lois Johnston

Second Edition

ON A COUNTRY ROAD

Bicycling is not a risk-free activity. Factors such as weather, road conditions, traffic and other hazards are in a constant state of change. Bicyclists choosing to attempt the tours described in this guidebook should follow safety standards and the state vehicle code, and use good judgment. The authors and publisher of this book can assume no liability for the risks inherent in this sport.

Photos by the authors

Published by: Greenways Press
                421 Centre Avenue
                Jeffersonville, PA 19403-3222

                ISBN: 0-9678446-0-6

Printed in the United States by:
Morris Publishing
3212 East Highway 30
Kearney, NE 68847
1-800-650-7888

Dedicated to our parents, Marian and Kenneth Johnston, and Dorothy and John DeHart, for the encouragement that led us down our first country roads many years ago.

Ride Locations

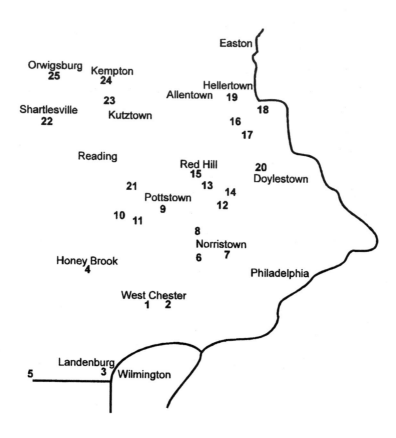

Contents

Preface To The Second Edition

When the 1st edition of *On A Country Road* was published, we were very pleased that the cycling community quickly embraced the new guide. On a cold Saturday in February of 1998, Lois and I shifted gears from book writers to book sellers. We threw a carton of our freshly printed books in the trunk of our car and, after a hearty breakfast at Mal's American Diner in Skippack, headed out to the bicycle shops. The shop owners we spoke with that morning recognized our publication as something their customers would ask for, and by the middle of the afternoon our books were proudly being displayed in three bicycle shops serving the North Penn and Indian Valleys. We thought three retailers was just grand for the first try, so we declared victory and went home. But in the weeks and months to come, our outlets multiplied and the idea of selling 500 copies became a reality.

In the spring and summer of 1999, we diligently began to plan the five new rides that we wanted to showcase in the 2nd edition. Once the new rides were in place, I took advantage of the lovely autumn weather and rode every route from the 1st edition, making sure the roads were still suitable. Seeing the entire southeastern region of Pennsylvania from Nottingham Park to Orwigsburg in a compressed period of only a few weeks helped me to realize how privileged we are to live in such a diverse and lively part of America.

It was especially fun to ride through the Amish country during the harvest season. A change in my career path gave me less time to ride on weekends, but more time during the week. Watching the farmers bring in their crops by horse and wagon really gave me the true flavor of this fascinating section of our region. It was also a joy to ride through the upper parts of Bucks County during the height of the fall foliage. Despite a serious summer drought, the colors were just as vivid as ever.

I would like to thank the members of the Montgomery County Community College Writers' Club, as well as the Community Writers of Montgomery County, for carefully critiquing many of the narratives included with each ride. I would also like to thank Phyllis L. Neumann, author of *Marin County Bike Trails,* for making suggestions on how we could improve our maps. Last, but not least, I would like to express my appreciation to the numerous innkeepers, historical site staff and merchants who took precious time away from their work to provide us with information that will be helpful to our readers.

Barry Johnston
Jeffersonville, PA
November 1999

Introduction

Much of southeastern Pennsylvania has become a series of rapidly developing suburban communities, complete with tract housing, shopping malls and business parks. However, with a little planning and a little luck, the pastoral scenery that once was typical of the region can still be discovered. Evansburg and French Creek State Parks challenge the hiker, while Valley Forge and Hopewell Village delight the history buff. Collectors of antiques flock to Skippack and Shartlesville, and bird watchers pursue their hobby at Peace Valley Park and Hawk Mountain.

Although this book gives a few hints on pursuing these interests, the main focus is on enjoying southeastern Pennsylvania's back roads by bicycle. We identified twenty-five routes, each highlighting a uniquely beautiful and historic part of the region. While intensive efforts to write this book began in 1996, learning about the roads took much longer. For example, the ride featuring the Orwigsburg and Hawk Mountain areas retraces routes used by one of the authors as he cycled to visit friends prior to getting a driver's license in the early 1970s. The ride leaving Lake Towhee in upper Bucks County is a variation of an after-work fitness ride used by one of the authors. The rides leaving West Chester are modifications of routes used by a charity bike tour the authors coordinated for a number of years.

Except for an extremely challenging road up Hawk Mountain, optional on the Kempton ride, we planned the routes to avoid too many arduous climbs. However, southeastern Pennsylvania is surprisingly hilly and we found it impossible to design a completely flat ride. On the contrary, we labeled many of the routes "hilly." It just seemed as if the most scenic routes in southeastern

Pennsylvania are in the highlands of the region. Riding a multiple speed bicycle greatly improves the enjoyment of these routes.

We also made efforts to obtain a reasonable geographical balance. One of the goals of the book was to offer rides within a two hour driving time of Philadelphia's City Hall. However we found some rides outside this radius that were just too pretty to eliminate. For example, the rides leaving Nottingham and Honeybrook provide excellent opportunities to view Pennsylvania's famous Amish country without traveling to the more tourist-oriented central Lancaster County area. Likewise, we just had to include a route in the Shartlesville area, where the reader can replenish lost calories at a genuine "all you can eat" Pennsylvania Dutch restaurant. Nonetheless, it is conceivable to take an early morning drive to any of the routes, enjoy a day of cycling and be back in Chestnut Hill or Bryn Mawr in time for dinner.

The last thing we want this book to be is a political statement. However, when cycling in one of these few remaining rural areas, one can't help wondering how to preserve what is left before southeastern Pennsylvania becomes more developed and commercialized. Nature trusts and open space purchases have certainly helped to preserve the countryside. Still, more needs to be done, including helping the local farm families preserve their businesses, not to mention their heritage. We need to start now if we want to keep the back roads of southeastern Pennsylvania enjoyable for bicycling and other outdoor pursuits.

Each ride described in this book is accompanied by a detailed cue sheet and a map showing the route and major cross roads. Points of interest and food stops are noted. Following each ride is a list of telephone numbers for the restaurants and attractions mentioned, as well as information on the nearest bicycle shops. It should be noted, however, that due to the rural nature of some ride locations, the nearest bicycle shop may actually be a number of miles away.

Tips For Safe Bicycling

Bicycling is not a risk-free sport and injuries can occur even to experienced cyclists. There are many factors involved, including the cyclist's skill, road conditions, cars, dogs, the weather, etc. We recommend that the following safety tips be followed, no matter what the skill level of the cyclist may be.

1. Wear a helmet. Approved helmets can lessen or prevent head injuries in the event of a fall.
2. Be sure your bicycle is in good repair.
3. Carry water to avoid dehydration.
4. Obey all the rules of the road.
5. Ride in single file, on the right side of the road.
6. Cross railroad tracks at a right angle.
7. Do not ride after dark unless your bicycle is equipped with appropriate lights.
8. Slow down and use extra caution if the road is wet, sandy, has loose gravel on it, or has potholes.
9. Signal turns in advance and be cautious when making left turns.
10. Stay in control of your bicycle.

A Special Note on Bridges

We cyclists have a special love for covered bridges. We love to see them along our routes and we love to ride through them. They are part of the ambiance that makes rural Pennsylvania so special. However, riding through a covered bridge can be dangerous if you are not familiar with the bridge's construction. Many of the covered bridges on our rides contain a riding surface consisting on long wooden planks that follow the length of the structure. Cracks between the planks eat bicycle tires, especially skinny racing designs! When in doubt, walk your bike through the bridge. Remember that drivers of automobiles may not see you as well inside a covered bridge as they would in normal daylight.

Bridges with a steel or iron surface normally do not pose a problem for the experienced cyclist. However, the feeling is a little odd the first time you cross such a bridge. All cyclists, regardless of ability, need to use extreme caution on an iron or steel bridge in wet weather.

Notable Bicycle Events In Southeastern Pennsylvania

Southeastern Pennsylvania plays host to a variety of events each year, attracting cyclists from all over the tri-state area. We cannot list all of them, but here are a few that seem to have withstood the test of time.

Taxing Metric Century
Hosted by the Brandywine Bicycle Club, the routes feature the hilly countryside of northern Chester County. The ride is usually held – when else? – the weekend closest to the April 15 income tax day. Keeping with the theme, the routes are generally marked with dollar signs. Contact the club at PO Box 3162, West Chester, PA 19381.

The (What's Left of) Open Space Tour
Until 1999, this event was known as the Freedom Tour. Sponsored by the Delaware Valley Bicycle Club, the rides begin at Ridley Creek State Park and feature parts of Delaware and Chester Counties where open space still exists. Contact the club at PO Box 156, Woodlyn, PA 19094.

Montgomery County Mexican Metric Century
Usually held in early May, the ride commemorates the Mexican Independence Day. Hosted by Suburban Cyclists Unlimited, Mexican food is offered at the rest stops. Contact the club at PO Box 401, Horsham, PA 19044.

Freedom Valley Bike Ride

An early June ride, this event is sponsored by the Bicycle Coalition of the Delaware Valley. The coalition is one of the premier advocacy organizations in the region. Contact BCDV on the Web at http://www.libertynet.org/~bcdv/.

Roll & Stroll

This ride benefits the Indian Creek Foundation, a human service agency providing opportunities for people with developmental disabilities to live in and enrich their communities in western Montgomery and Bucks counties. Usually held in mid to late June, the ride meanders through Upper Perkiomen and Indian Creek Valleys. Sag support is provided by local bicycle shops. A fantastic lunch, entertainment and massages are available after the ride. Contact Indian Creek Foundation at PO Box 225, Harleysville, PA 19438 or phone (215)256-6156.

Lutheran Charities Steeple Chase Bike Ride

This ride includes tours of 18 to 100 miles on the beautiful roads of central and western Montgomery County, and is usually held in late June. Using Lutheran Churches as rest stops, the ride features some of the friendliest volunteers you'll ever meet. A unique feature of the ride is the addition of two Lutheran ministers on motorcycles as part of the sag support. A welcoming hot dog party greets the riders at the start-finish point. For information, contact Lutheran Charities at Ken-Crest, (610)825-9360.

USPRO Cycling Championships-Liberty Classic

Early June affords the opportunity of the year to watch the top professional racers strut their stuff in Philadelphia. For early risers, a local charity usually sponsors a ride for non-racers a few hours before the event. It is a great opportunity to ride the famous course and savor the rich variety of neighborhoods that make up the great city of Philadelphia.

Scenic Schuylkill Century

Held around the middle of September, this relative newcomer has gained a popular following rather quickly. The ride begins in

Philadelphia and takes the rider into the beautiful hills of northern Chester County. The ride ends with a festive pizza party in Fairmount Park, where live music and massages are available. For information, contact the Bicycle Club of Philadelphia on the Internet at info@phillybikeclub.org.

Lake Nockamixon Century

Beginning in Horsham, this ride provides a unique opportunity to view the transformation from suburban to rural countryside as one rides from central into upper Bucks County. It is usually held in late September. Contact Suburban Cyclists Unlimited at PO Box 401, Horsham, PA 19044.

Covered Bridges Ride

The Central Bucks Bicycle Club chose the month of October for this event in order to highlight the colorful foliage of rural Bucks County. Up to eight covered bridges can be visited, each with it's own unique history and character. Contact the Central Bucks Bicycle Club at PO Box 1648, Doylestown, PA 18901.

Brandywine Country:
A Tour Of Central Chester County

- 23.6 miles
- Start and end at Everhart Park within the borough of West Chester
- Terrain: rolling

Highlights

- Roads along the famous Brandywine Creek
- Beautiful horse farms
- Embreeville Mill

The townships just south of West Chester are quintessential Chester County. The landscape is dominated by the meandering Brandywine Creek, with just enough horse farms to paint the countryside picture perfect. While new housing is denser than it was ten years ago, organizations such as the Brandywine Valley Association are doing their part to preserve this historical section of rural Pennsylvania.

West Chester itself is worth exploring if there is time after your ride. The borough is home to a fine state university with beautiful stone buildings situated at the older end of the campus. West Chester is also the county seat, with a downtown area containing many quaint shops and restaurants. Because of its many fine examples of Greek revival architecture, West Chester was once known as "the Athens of Pennsylvania."

Several food stops are noted on the cue sheet. We personally recommend The Corner Store in the center of Unionville, 10.8 miles into the ride. Tim and Sissy Wickes purchased the property in 1998, converting the grocery store into a specialty market and café. With "good fresh food" as their motto, the Wickes offer a tempting collection of salads, in addition to superb gourmet sandwiches. Many of the Unionville area's horse enthusiasts like to stop in for a midday break, as do the veterinary staff from the nearby Bolton Center of the University of Pennsylvania. Please be careful walking inside the store with cleated bicycle shoes. The new owners have lovingly restored the store's original hardwood floor. The Corner Store is not open on Mondays.

Getting to Everhart Park

West Chester itself is very accessible from the greater Philadelphia area. Route 202 and Route 3 are the main roads between Philadelphia and West Chester. Once inside the borough, take Gay Street down to North New Street. Make a left turn onto North New Street, cross Market Street and make a right turn onto Miner Street. Everhart Park is a few blocks down on the left. The intersection of Brandywine and Miner Streets forms the northwest corner of the park.

The Ride

0.0	L	From the corner of South Brandywine (on the side of the park) and Miner Streets, make a left turn onto Miner Street.
0.2	S	Leaving the borough of West Chester, cross Bradford Avenue. Miner Street becomes Route 842 west.
1.7	BL	Bear left, staying on Route 842.

3.1	R	Make a right turn, staying on Route 842. Immediately cross the Brandywine Creek.
4.0	L	Make a left turn, staying on Route 842. Again cross the Brandywine Creek.
4.1	L	Make a left turn onto Wawaset Road.
4.2	S	Caution. Cross railroad tracks at right angle. Begin to climb a hill, reaching the crest at 4.7 miles.
6.0	L	Make a left turn, staying on Wawaset Road.
6.5	R	Make a right turn onto Lenape Unionville Road. Do not miss this turn, as a straight will put you on busy Route 52! The county-administered Pocopson Home is on your left.
8.3	BL	Bear left, staying on Lenape Unionville Road.
9.5	R	Make a right turn onto East Doe Run Road.
9.75	BL	Bear left, staying on East Doe Run Road.
10.1	R	Make a right turn onto Unionville Road (Route 82). Caution: busy road! Enter village of Unionville. The Corner Store will be on the right just before you turn onto Embreeville Road.
10.8	R	Make a right turn onto Embreeville Road.
12.8	BR	Bear right, staying on Embreeville Road.
13.6	S	Pass a KOA Campground on the left.
15.0	R	Make a right turn onto Brandywine Drive. Embreeville Center is on the left, just before making the turn.
17.3	BL	Bear left at the stop sign. Immediately pass Castle Rock Farm.
18.1	R	Make a right turn onto Camp Linden Road.
18.8	R	Make a right turn onto North Wawaset Road.
19.6	L	Make a left turn onto Route 842.

20.1	BR	Bear right, staying on Route 842.
20.5	L	Make a left turn, staying on Route 842.
23.4	S	Straight at stop sign.
23.6	END	End at Miner and South Brandywine Streets.

FYI

The Corner Store, Unionville (610-347-2225)

Bicycle Shops

Bike Line, West Goshen Shopping Center, West Chester, PA (610-436-8984)

Bike Line, 404 West Lincoln Highway, Exton, PA (610-594-9380)

Exton Bicycles, 315 East Lincoln Highway, Exton, PA (610-363-2747)

West Chester Bicycle Center, 1342 West Chester Pike, West Chester, PA (610-431-1856)

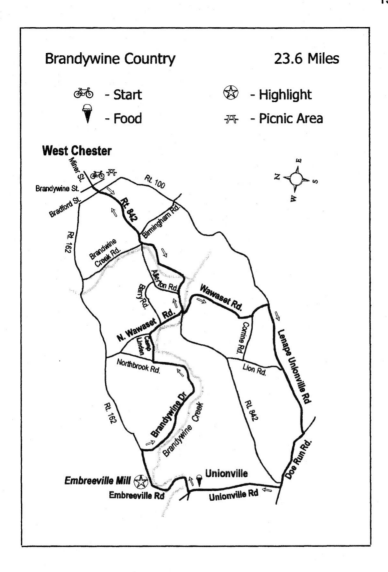

Brandywine Country   23.6 Miles

🚲 - Start   ✪ - Highlight
🍦 - Food   🪑 - Picnic Area

West Chester

Plenty of horses can be seen along Chester County's rural roads.

Artists' Paradise:
The Farmlands of Chester County

- 48.7 miles
- Start and end at Everhart Park, within the borough of West Chester
- Terrain: rolling with a few steep uphills

Highlights

- Beautiful horse farms.
- Roads along the famous Brandywine Creek.
- Embreeville Mill.
- Covered bridge
- Historic Primitive Hall
- Brandywine Valley Association

Do you want to see the finest horse farms east of Kentucky? The central and western townships of Chester County contain the prettiest horse farms that we have ever seen. No wonder that artists such as the Wyeths have made their homes in this unique part of Pennsylvania. Meandering through the area is Brandywine Creek. The waterway is too small and shallow for anything larger than a canoe or kayak, but it is big enough to be a major attraction for those seeking pastoral beauty.

The ride itself is a longer version of "Brandywine Country." As stated in the opening remarks to that ride, we recommend that you spend some time exploring West Chester itself. The borough contains a fine University, with interesting architecture inside the older section of the campus. The shopping district is home to many fine restaurants and interesting shops, as well as the stately county courthouse.

As on the shorter ride, The Corner Store in Unionville is the recommended lunch stop. Please read the appropriate section in "Brandywine Country" to find out more about this unique eatery.

Getting to Everhart Park

West Chester itself is very accessible from the greater Philadelphia area. Route 202 and Route 3 are the main roads between Philadelphia and West Chester. Once inside the borough, take Gay Street down to North New Street. Make a left turn onto North New Street, cross Market Street and make a right turn onto Miner Street. Everhart Park is a few blocks down on the left. The intersection of Brandywine and Miner Streets forms the northwest corner of the park.

The Ride

0.0	L	From the corner of South Brandywine (on the side of the park) and Miner Streets, make a left turn onto Miner Street.
0.2	S	Leaving the borough of West Chester, cross Bradford Ave. Miner Street becomes Route 842 west.
1.7	BL	Bear left, staying on Route 842.
3.1	R	Make a right turn, staying on Route 842. Immediately cross the Brandywine Creek.
4.0	S	Go straight. Route 842 will turn left. You are now on North Wawaset Road.
4.8	L	Turn left onto Camp Linden Road.

5.5	L	Make a left turn at T onto Northbrook Road (unmarked). When the turn is made, there will be horse pastures on either side of the road and a farm ahead.
6.3	R	Make a right turn onto Brandywine Drive. This is a very scenic, but narrow road. Watch for traffic.
8.65	L	Make a left turn onto Route 162 (unmarked). After making the turn Embreeville Center will be on the left side of the road. At one time, this was an institution for people with mental retardation. However, the center officially closed in 1997, and the buildings and grounds now have multiple uses. For instance, many of the fields are now used for soccer leagues.
9.4	S	Straight at stop sign, staying on Route 162 (also known as Embreeville Road).
10.0	S	Pass a KOA Campground on right. Use caution at the railroad tracks.
10.3	S	Pass the Embreeville Mill, a favorite subject of local artists.
10.75	R	Make a right onto Powell Road.
10.8	R	Make a right turn onto Brandywine Creek Road.
11.9	R	Make a right turn onto an unmarked (and un-named) road. Immediately cross a very scenic concrete bridge.
12.0	L	Make a left turn onto Youngs Road (the sign pointing the opposite direction will say "Harvey's Bridge Road").
12.1	L	Make a left turn onto Laurel Road.
14.2	S	Cross Strasburg Road. Laurel Road becomes Mortonville Road. Find food and drink at Marty's Pub on right.

15.0	L	Make a left turn , staying on Mortonville Road. (The road sign says "Mortonville Road," but local maps show this as Creek Road).
16.4	L	Inside the little borough of Modena, make a left turn onto Union Street. Use caution. A stone wall on the left makes it a little hard to see up the road.
16.5	L	Make a left turn onto South Brandywine Avenue.
16.55	R	Make a right turn onto Hephzibah Road. Ascend the steepest hill of the ride.
17.35	R	Make a right turn onto Strasburg Road.
17.4	L	Make a left turn onto Frog Hollow Road (local maps show this as "Hephzibah Hill Road"). Houdeeney's Pizza is on the corner. After enjoying a pizza, enjoy a downhill almost two miles long!
19.2	S	Cross a covered bridge. Caution! The floor of this bridge is VERY uneven. When we were affiliated with a charity ride that used this road, we used to make cyclists walk through the bridge because of the uneven flooring.
19.2	L	After going through the bridge, make a left turn onto Covered Bridge Road.
19.6	R	Make a right turn onto Dupont Road .
19.8	L	Make a left turn onto Doe Run Road (Route 82). Caution: busy road.
20.3	R	Make a right turn onto Route 841 south (Chatham Road).
20.5	R	Make a right turn onto Chapel Road.
21.3	S	Go straight at the stop sign.
22.5	BL	Bear left onto Gum Tree Road. Do NOT make the sharp left turn onto Rosenvick Road. Enter the tiny village of Gum Tree.

23.2	R	Make a right turn onto Friendship Church Road.
25.3	L	Make a left turn onto Friends Meetinghouse Road (unmarked). Caution: this road is easy to miss because it is unmarked. A little further up Friendship Church Road is a stop sign and an intersection with a busy road. This is Route 10. If you are here, go back. You went too far.
26.8	S	Go straight at the stop sign.
27.1	L	Make a left turn at the Y, staying on Friends Meetinghouse Road.
27.9	BR	Bear right.
28.7	L	Make a left turn onto Green Lawn Road.
30.4	R	Make a right turn onto North Chatham Road.
31.2	S	Go straight, staying on Route 841 South. Pass historical Primitive Hall on left. Primitive Hall is a large Georgian country house built in 1738.
31.9	BR	Bear right.
32.0	L	Make a left turn onto Route 926 (Street Road).
32.8	R	Make a right turn onto Howellmoore Road.
33.75	L	Make a left turn onto London Grove Road.
35.1	L	Make a left turn onto Spencer Road. Pass the Stroud Water Research Center on left.
36.2	L	Left onto Newark Road.
36.5	S	Go straight at the stop sign.
37.6	R	Make a right turn onto Upland Road (Route 842).
39.65	R	Make a right turn, staying on Route 842. Enter the village of Unionville.
39.9	S	The Corner Store is on the left. Use caution if you decide to cross the road to visit the store.
40.0	L	Make a left turn, staying on Route 842 (Wawaset Road).

42.9	S	Pass Northbrook Orchards on the left. Refreshments can be purchased anytime, but it is really worthwhile stopping in during the harvest season. Try a cider donut!
43.2	S	Pass the Brandywine Valley Association. Often there are special events going on here on weekends. It is worth the stop.
44.5	S	Caution. Cross the railroad track at a right angle.
44.6	BL	Bear left, crossing the bridge over the creek.
44.7	R	Make a right turn, staying on Route 842.
45.2	BR	Bear right.
45.6	L	Make a left turn, staying on Route 842.
48.5	S	Go straight at the stop sign.
48.7	END	End ride at the corner of Miner and South Brandywine Streets.

FYI

Brandywine Valley Association, West Chester (610-793-1090)
Northbrook Orchards, West Chester (610-793-1210)
The Corner Store, Unionville (610-347-2225)

Bicycle Shops

Bike Line, West Goshen Shopping Center, West Chester, PA (610-436-8984)

Exton Bicycles, 315 East Lincoln Highway, Exton, PA (610-363-2747)

West Chester Bicycle Center, 1342 West Chester Pike, West Chester, PA (610-431-1856)

Artists' Paradise — 48.7 Miles

🚲 - Start ✪ - Highlight 🍴 - Picnic Area 🍦 - Food

The Far Southeast Corner:
The White Clay and Big Elk Creeks

- 25.9 miles
- Start and end at the White Clay Creek Preserve
- Rolling hills

Highlights

- Whiteclay Creek Preserve
- Chester County farm country
- Beautiful Big Elk Creek
- Quaint village of Landenberg
- Cornerstone Bed and Breakfast

In 1984, the Dupont Corporation donated a sizable tract of land to form the White Clay Creek Preserve. This generous gift enabled the Pennsylvania Bureau of State Parks (as well as its counterpart in the State of Delaware) to preserve the area's unique ecosystem, as well as the many structures of historical interest. While modern-day housing development is very evident between the twelve and nineteen mile marks of the ride, much of the ride travels through woods and farmland that gives you a hint of what a very young commonwealth might have looked like at the beginning of the 19th century.

The oldest settlement in the area was probably Opasiskunk, a Lenapi village covering several acres. The oldest European dwelling within the preserve is the Yeatman Mill House, which is believed to have been the center of the region's milling industry.

An interesting site right along the route is the London Tract Baptist Meeting House, built in 1729.

After leaving the White Clay Creek Preserve, you head west and then north towards the West Grove/Avondale area. The scenery on this part of the ride (besides the housing developments) highlights the area's more recent history, especially its contributions to agriculture. In the last few decades, Avondale and the surrounding townships figured prominently in the mushroom industry. In total darkness, mushrooms grow in long cinder "houses" that you can occasionally see along the ride route. You might also spot greenhouses as you travel along the route. Within these glass enclosures, the cultivation of roses takes place, the finest of which are sold to floral shops across the region.

Just before finishing the ride, you ride through the tiny village of Landenburg. The store on the left contains a selection of sandwiches in its deli section, as well as groceries. Along the walls of the store are some rather interesting photographs of the village in much earlier times. When we rode through the area in the fall of 1999, we discovered that the entire village was for sale. We also learned that the historic Landenberg bridge was out and a grass roots effort was being organized to reconstruct this community landmark.

The Cornerstone Bed and Breakfast, a lovely weathered fieldstone home, sits on the corner of Buttonwood and Newark Roads, 1.2 miles from the start of the ride. The original house dates back to the early 1700's and has been enlarged over the years. Today, elegant rooms are decorated with 18th century pieces to delight and remind you of the gracious style of an earlier era. Be sure to look for the elaborate mantels which were made by former Hessian soldiers after the War for Independence.

Getting to the White Clay Creek Preserve

From Philadelphia, take Route 1 south, past Kennett Square, to the Toughkenamon exit. Turn left at the end of the ramp onto Newark Road. At the corner of Buttonwood and Newark Road, you will see Cornerstone Bed and Breakfast. Make a right turn onto Buttonwood Road. After half a mile, make another right turn onto Broad Run Road. Travel another half a mile and bear left onto London Tract Road. Shortly, you will see Parking Lot #1 on your left.

The Ride

0.0	L	Begin at Parking Lot #1 on London Tract Road. With your back toward the parking lot, make a left turn onto London Tract Road.
1.2	L	Make a left turn, staying on London Tract Road. Look for the road after you cross a little bridge. The sign may be obscured by foliage.
1.9	R	Make a sharp right turn, staying on London Tract Road. The London Tract Baptist Meeting House is on the left at this intersection.
2.2	BL	Bear left, staying on London Tract Road.
3.3	S	Go straight, crossing Route 896. Caution: busy road.
4.2	S	Go straight. London Tract Road becomes Strickersville Road.
5.0	S	Straight, staying on Strickersville Road.
7.8	R	Make a right turn onto Route 841.
9.2	S	Where Route 841 bears right, continue straight onto Lewisville Road.

9.5	BR	Bear right, staying on Lewisville Road.
10.7	L	Make a left turn, staying on Lewisville Road.
11.9	R	Make a right turn onto State Road.
12.3	S	Straight, crossing Route 896. The Jack in the Pulpit gift shop is on the right.
16.0	S	Straight, crossing Wickerton Road.
16.9	R	Make a right turn onto Rose Hill Road.
17.9	R	Make a right turn onto Avondale Road.
18.6	S	Go straight, staying on Avondale Road.
19.0	L	Make a left turn onto Wickerton Road (Route 841).
19.8	R	Make a right turn staying on Route 841.
20.6	L	Make a left turn onto Chesterville Road. The sign may be obscured.
21.2	BR	Cross a bridge and bear right.
22.0	BL	Bear left, staying on Chesterville Road.
22.2	L	Make a left turn onto North Bank Road.
22.8	R	Make a right turn onto Auburn Road.
22.9	S	Straight, staying on Auburn Road.
23.7	R	Make a right turn onto Penn Green Road.
24.9	S	Continue straight through the village of Landenberg. The Landenberg store will be on your left.
25.5	L	Make a left turn onto Good Hope Road.
25.7	R	Make a right turn onto London Tract Road.
25.9	END	End at Parking Lot #1 on London Tract Road.

FYI

Cornerstone Bed and Breakfast, Landenberg (610-274-2143)
White Clay Creek Preserve, Landenberg (610-255-5415)

Bicycle Shops

Bike Line, West Goshen Shopping Center, West Chester, PA (619-436-8984)

Bike Line, 2900 N. Concord Pike, Wilmington, DE (302-479-9438)

Bike Line, 212 E. Main Street, Newark, DE (302-368-8779)

Dunbar's Cyclery, 801 Phila. Pike, Wilmington, DE (302-764-5802)

West Chester Bicycle Center, 1342 West Chester Pike, West Chester (610-431-1856)

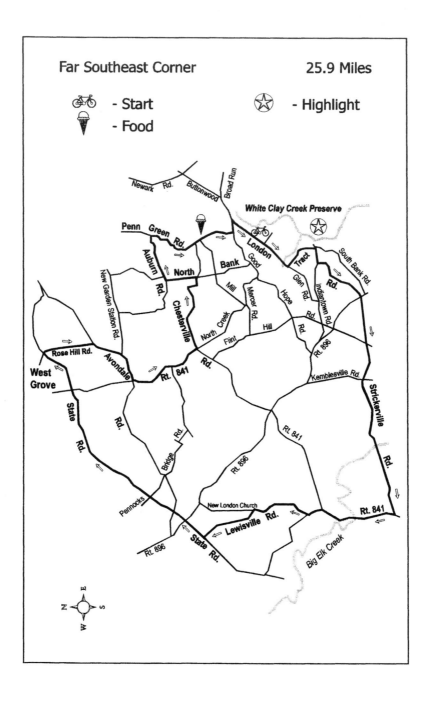

Far Southeast Corner   25.9 Miles

🚲 - Start   ⭐ - Highlight
🍦 - Food

A Honey Of A Ride:
Honeybrook And Lancaster County

- 18.8 miles
- Start and end by parking lot on Firehouse Lane, Honeybrook, across the street from the library and municipal building
- Terrain: hilly

Highlights

- Horse drawn carriages
- Beautiful Amish farm country
- Fassitt Mansion Bed and Breakfast
- Waynebrook Inn

Just like the Nottingham Park ride, this route starts in the rolling hills of Chester County and takes a quick dip into Lancaster County. The ride goes just far enough into Lancaster County to see all the pastoral scenery associated with this beautiful part of Pennsylvania. But, at the same time, the route stays well to the east of the area frequented by tour buses and heavy traffic.

Within the village of Honeybrook, there are a variety of places from which you can purchase food. Sometimes you may also find an impromptu food stand set up by an Amish family along the road.

If you are thinking of extending your stay, we offer two recommendations. The Waynebrook Inn, just across the street from the starting point of the ride, is a splendidly refurbished inn which was built in 1738. Throughout the years, the structure has functioned as either a tavern, an inn or a hotel.

A second option is the Fassitt Mansion Bed and Breakfast, an 1845 country mansion in nearby White Horse. The first owners to run the mansion as a Bed and Breakfast were bicycle enthusiasts who advertised their business in bicycle-related publications. Bill Collins, the current proprietor, describes himself as "a very happy innkeeper," as well as the proud owner of a Yamaha 1600 motorcycle.

Guests have the whole mansion to themselves, as Bill and his family live in the carriage house just in back of the main house. Each of the five rooms is furnished to complement the elegance of the historic home.

"We have a lot of cruiser clubs who stay here," Bill stated. "They are looking for the same back country roads as the bicyclists. A lot of times I will see them at the same intersection, looking at the same pretty pond or farm that the bicyclists stop and look at." Bill does all the cooking, priding himself on his hearty country breakfasts. If you are still hungry, Bill's homemade pies, cheesecakes and other goodies are available anytime.

The Fassitt Mansion Bed and Breakfast is located six-tenths of a mile from the intersection of Plank and Blank Roads, along the ride route. Instead of making a right turn onto Blank to follow the route, make a left turn onto Blank. Follow Blank Road three-tenths of a mile and make a left turn onto Old Philadelphia Pike (a somewhat busy road, so please use caution). Follow Old Philadelphia Pike another three-tenths of a mile to the Fassitt Mansion, a large white building on the left side of the road.

Getting to Honeybrook

Honeybrook can be reached by getting off the turnpike at Morgantown and taking Route 23 west to Route 10 south. An alternative from Philadelphia's western suburbs is to take Route 30 west to Route 322 west. The parking lot on Firehouse Lane can be seen from Route 10, a block south of the intersection of

Routes 10 and 322. Traveling south on Route 10, there are signs for the municipal building and the library on the right. The parking lot is on the left. Public parking is no longer permitted in this lot, but plenty of parking can be found on the side streets nearby.

The Ride

0.0	R	With your back to the parking lot on Firehouse Lane, turn right (corner of Firehouse Lane and Railroad Street).
0.15	R	Make a right turn onto Maple Street.
0.25	L	Make a left turn onto Park Street.
0.4	S	Go straight at the stop sign.
3.0	R	Turn right onto Beaver Dam Road.
4.95	S	Go straight at the stop sign.
6.8	BR	Bear right onto Byerly Road
7.55	L	Make a left turn onto Churchtown Road.
7.8	R	Make a right turn onto Plank Road.
8.6	R	Make a right turn onto Blank Road (no, this is not a typo. There actually is a Plank Road and a Blank Road).
10.3	L	Make a left turn onto Wanner Road.
10.9	L	Make a left turn onto Cambridge Road.
11.3	S	Go straight on Seldonridge Road (Cambridge Road bears left).
11.4	S	Go straight at the stop sign.
12.0	S	Go straight. Seldonridge becomes Meetinghouse Road.
12.6	R	Make a right turn onto Meadeville Road.
13.6	L	Make a left turn onto Gault Road.

13.65	R	Make a right turn onto Meadeville Road.
14.3	R	Make a right turn onto Meadeville Road.
17.4	R	Make a right turn onto West Walnut Road.
18.2	S	Cross Route 10. Caution. This is a busy inter-section.
18.35	L	Make a left turn onto Maple Street.
18.7	L	Make a left turn onto Firehouse Lane
18.85	END	End ride at the parking lot.

FYI

Fassitt Mansion Bed & Breakfast, White Horse (800-653-4139 or www.fassittmansion.com)
Waynebrook Inn, P.O. Box 610, Honeybrook (610-273-2444)

Bicycle Shops

Bike Line, Airport Village Shopping Center, Coatesville, PA (610-380-4553)

Bike Line, 117 Rohrerstown Road, Lancaster, PA (717-394-8998)

Downingtown Bicycle Shop, 833 West Lancaster Avenue, Downingtown, PA (610-269-5626)

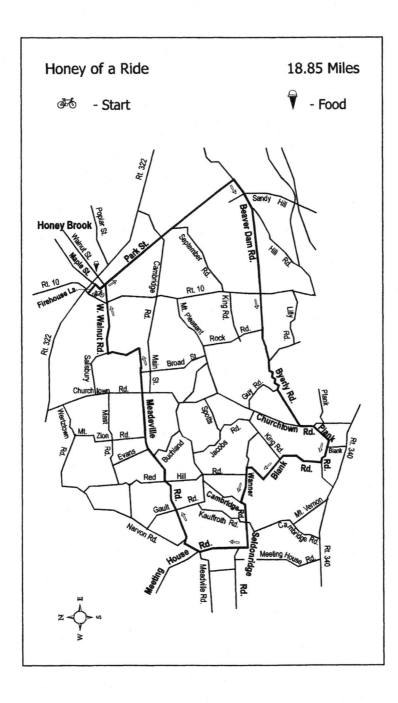

Honey of a Ride

18.85 Miles

🚲 - Start

🍦 - Food

Proof that Blank and Plank really are two different roads.

Potato Chips And Farmlands: Nottingham Park And Lancaster County

- 28.6 miles
- Start and end at Nottingham County Park
- Terrain: hilly

Highlights

- Nottingham County Park
- Horse-drawn carriages
- Beautiful Amish farm country
- Covered bridge
- One room schoolhouse
- Little Britain Manor Bed and Breakfast

Lancaster County has developed a much deserved reputation for bicycling. Its many rural roads wander through lush pastures, occasionally dotted with covered bridges and one room Amish schoolhouses. However, within the more popular areas, cyclists often need to share the road with tour buses and other seasonal traffic. This ride, as well as the ride leaving Honeybrook, explores the eastern tip of Lancaster County, which is a region that the tourists often miss.

Like the Honeybrook ride, your tour starts and ends in Chester County. Nottingham Township is famous as the home of Herr Foods, a popular provider of potato chips and other snack foods (free tours are available hourly at the factory on weekdays, complete with free samples of freshly made potato chips). The township's other prized possession is a lovely county park that draws more than 100,000 visitors each year. Its picnic pavilions are often used as food stops for local century rides coming through the park. The 651 acre park has a unique outcropping of serpentine stone, called the serpentine barrens, which is said to be one of the most unusual and rare ecosystems in the world. The park also features a lake, pond, and hiking trails.

If you would like to extend your stay in this unique part of the Commonwealth, a Bed and Breakfast called "Little Britain Manor" is located at the six mile mark of the ride. Innkeepers Fred and Evelyn Crider invite their guests to awaken to the aroma of coffee, eggs, bacon, homemade biscuits and sweet bologna. The inn boasts four bedrooms, each decorated in a distinctive country flavor.

You can purchase lunch and snack items within the tiny town of Little Britain, located at the intersection of Brown Road and Route 272 at 6.3 miles on the tour. We especially recommend the store's whoopee pies. Whoopee pies contain an icing-like filling between two small round chocolate cakes. We have only found this tantalizing treat in Lancaster County and along the Maine coast, and both of these areas claim to have "invented" the whoopee pie.

Getting to Nottingham County Park

Nottingham County Park is most easily reached from the Philadelphia area by taking Route 1 to the Nottingham Exit, just south of Oxford, PA. After exiting Route 1, follow the brown and white signs for Nottingham County Park. The main gate is on Park Road on the left. The ride begins at the main gate.

The Ride

0.0	L	From the main gate, make a left turn onto Park Road.
1.5	S	Continue straight after stop sign. Park road becomes Lee's Bridge Road. Watch for traffic coming from right.
1.9	R	Make a right turn onto Freemont Road.
3.3	BL	Cross the Lancaster County Line. Bear left after crossing bridge.
4.3	S	Continue straight on Freemont Road, which becomes Brown Road. Pass the Little Britain Manor on left at 6.0 miles.
6.3	S	Straight, crossing Route 272. Brown Road becomes Little Britain (North) Road.
7.4	R	Make a right turn onto Jackson Road.
8.1	BR	Bear right staying on Jackson Road (unmarked). Sign for road ahead says "Spring Hill Road."
8.4	R	Make a right turn at the T (unmarked).
8.8	L	Make a left turn onto Shady 337 Road.
9.4	L	Make a left turn onto King Pen Road.
10.0	S	Stay on King Pen Road, following sign saying, "covered bridge ahead."
10.2	R	Make a right turn, going through the covered bridge.
10.4	BL	Bear left onto White Rock Road.
11.4	R	Make a right turn onto Hill Road. Pass Amish one room schoolhouse on left.
11.7	S	Straight, staying on Hill Road.
11.9	R	Make a right turn onto Street Road. Caution: traffic on left is coming over the crest of a hill.

12.8	L	Make a left turn onto Kirkwood Pike (Route 472).
13.0	R	Make the first right turn onto Morrison Mill Road. The sign is partially obscured.
13.4	R	Make a right turn onto Sproul Road.
14.6	R	Make a right turn onto Rosedale Road.
15.4	L	Make a left turn onto Street Road.
16.6	R	Make a right turn onto Newcomer's Road.
17.1	R	Make a right turn at the T onto Homeville Road (unmarked).
18.25	R	Make a right turn onto Cream Road (unmarked). On the right are the Cream Gift Shop and Robert Trent Hogge, Cabinetmaker. The gift shop is worth visiting.
19.1	L	Make a left turn onto Scroggy Road (unmarked).
19.95	R	Make a right turn onto Jackson School Road.
20.2	BL	Bear left, staying on Jackson School Road. Enjoy a long downhill!
21.25	L	Make a left turn onto Lancaster Pike (unmarked). Caution: busy road. A reservoir will be on the right.
21.4	R	Make a sharp right onto Bethel Road. Local maps may call this "Mt. Vernon Road."
22.5	BL	Bear left at the stop sign, staying on Bethel Road.
22.9	R	Make a right turn onto Street Road.
23.6	L	Make a left turn at the T onto Forge Road (unmarked).
25.05	R	Make a right turn onto Hopewell Road (unmarked). This is the first right turn past Calvary Road.

26.25	L	Make a left turn onto Glen Roy Road. Immediately cross Route 272.
27.1	S	Straight, staying on Glen Roy Road.
28.0	R	Make a right turn onto Cemetery Road.
28.35	L	Make a left turn onto Park Road.
28.6	END	End ride at main gate of Nottingham County Park.

FYI

Herr Foods, Nottingham (800-284-7488)
Little Britain Manor, Little Britain (717-529-2862)
Nottingham County Park, Nottingham (610-932-9195)

Bicycle Shops

Bike Line, 212 East Main Street, Newark, DE (302-368-8779)

Bike Line, 117 Rohrerstown Road, Lancaster, PA (717-394-8998)

46

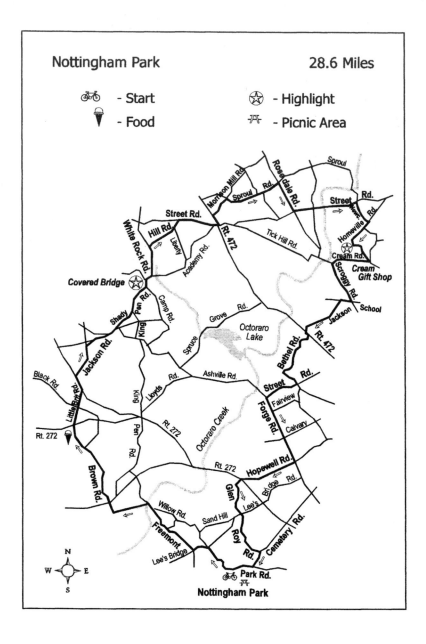

Where Old Meets New:
Valley Forge and Chesterbrook

- 15.3 miles, with up to 44 additional miles possible on bikeway
- Start and end at the Betzwood Picnic Area of Valley Forge National Historical Park
- Terrain: rolling, but optional trip on bikeway is flat

Highlights

- Valley Forge National Historical Park
- Great Valley Mill
- Knox Covered Bridge
- Diamond Rock Octagonal School
- Philadelphia to Valley Forge Bikeway
- Accessible by rail from Philadelphia

Valley Forge is well known for its place in American history. It was here that George Washington and his army survived, barely, the bitter winter of 1777-78. Today, the extensive remains and reconstructions bring the dramatic story to life for the many visitors to the National Historical Park. The park is also a beautiful place of hills and meadows, with hiking trails, picnic areas, and a six mile bike path around the perimeter. We recommend a stop at the Visitor Center, and, if time permits, a tour of the park by car or bicycle.

The ride passes by Diamond Rock School at the 6.6 mile point. This structure is one of five octagonal schools built in the region during the early 1800's. It is constructed of stone, and measures ten feet to each of the eight sides. At the 7.5 mile point, the ride passes Great Valley Mill. Historical records indicate that a mill has stood at this spot since 1710, and the current structure was erected in 1859 by Joseph E. Jeanes . It was in active service as late as 1950.

From the historic Valley Forge area, the ride continues into Chesterbrook, a modern planned community of four thousand homes. With a shopping center and a number of high-tech industries, Chesterbrook is a model of a self-contained community.

Food is available on the ride at stores and restaurants in the Chesterbrook Village Center, at the ten mile point in the ride. Tables and grills are located in the Betzwood Picnic Area, at the start/finish point.

You may extend the length of the ride by turning right instead of left on the Schuylkill River Trail at the end of the ride. This Philadelphia to Valley Forge bikeway follows the Schuylkill River through Norristown, Conshohocken, and Spring Mill to Manayunk. It detours onto Manayunk streets for a short way, and then continues along Kelly Drive all the way to the Philadelphia Art Museum. The scenery includes everything from forested parks and outstanding river vistas to suburban neighborhoods and heavy industrial sites. You may travel as far as you wish before turning around and retracing your route back to the Betzwood Picnic Area. The distance to Philadelphia from Valley Forge on the Schuylkill River Trail is 22 miles.

Getting to Valley Forge

From Philadelphia, take either the Pennsylvania Turnpike or the Schuylkill Expressway to King of Prussia, and get on Route 422 west. Continue on Route 422 to the exit for Route 363 (Trooper Road). Make a left turn onto Trooper Road at the end of the exit ramp, continue across the overpass, and turn right into the Betzwood Picnic Area.

Parking is also available at the lower lot behind the Visitor Center in the park. Reach it from Route 422 by following the signs for Valley Forge Park. Exit the parking lot on the right side by walking around the gate, and make a left onto County Line Road, joining the ride at the .7 mile point.

Recently, SEPTA has allowed bicycles on its rail lines during off-peak hours. To access the ride using SEPTA, take the R6 train to the Norristown Transportation Center. The Schuylkill River Trail passes right by the station. Cycle this bikeway west 4 miles to the Betzwood Picnic Area.

The Ride

0.0	S	Exit the Betzwood parking lot by following the paved bike path, which begins next to the bulletin board.
0.05	R	Make a right turn on the bike path, following the sign for the river crossing.
0.3	L	Make a left turn after leaving the bridge across the Schuylkill River, following the bikeway signs.
0.5	R	Make a right turn at stop sign onto Route 23. Caution: busy road!
0.5	L	Make an immediate left turn onto County Line Road (unmarked). A sign points to "Maintenance Area." Fences along part of County Line Road mark an asbestos removal area, so please stay on the roadway.

Optional: To visit the Visitor Center, turn left at the beginning of County Line Road onto the bike path. Travel on the bike path about .5 mile to the Visitor Center on the right. If you would like to see a bit more of the park, continue past the Visitor Center on the bike path until you reach the National Memorial Arch. Just past the Arch, turn left onto Outer Line Drive, rejoining the ride at the 2.0 mile point. Caution: the bike path in the park is popular with walkers and runners, and tends to be crowded on weekends.

1.9	L	Make a left turn at the T onto North Gulph Road (unmarked).
2.0	R	Make a right turn onto Outer Line Drive, just before the National Memorial Arch. Outer Line Drive parallels the bike path.
3.6	R	Make a right turn at the stop sign onto Route 252.
4.0	L	Make a left turn, going through Knox Covered Bridge and onto Yellow Springs Road.
6.6	S	Pass Diamond Rock School on the right.
6.7	BL	Bear left onto North Valley Road.
7.5	S	Pass Great Valley Mill on the left.
7.7	L	Make a left turn onto Swedesford Road.
8.5	L	Make a left turn at the traffic light onto Duportail Road.
9.5	L	Make a left turn at the traffic light onto Chesterbrook Boulevard.
11.2	S	Continue straight at the traffic light onto Sullivan Road.
11.5	L	Make a left turn at the T onto Anthony Wayne Drive.
11.6	R	Make a right turn at the stop sign onto Walker Road (unmarked).
12.1	L	Make a left turn at the stop sign onto Thomas Road.
13.0	L	Make a left turn at the T onto North Gulph Road. Reenter Valley Forge National Historical Park. Use caution on the bricks by the National Memorial Arch.

13.5	R	Make a right turn onto County Line Road (unmarked).
14.8	R	Make a right turn onto Route 23.
14.8	L	Make an immediate left turn onto an unmarked road. Follow the river crossing signs.
15.0	R	Make a right turn onto the bikeway to cross the river.
15.25	L	Make a left turn onto the bikeway and follow it to the parking area.

Optional: To extend the ride, turn right rather than left onto the Schuylkill River Trail. The bikeway can be followed for as long as desired, and continues for 22 flat miles to Philadelphia.

| 15.3 | END | End at Betzwood Picnic Area. |

FYI

Valley Forge National Historical Park, Valley Forge (610-783-1077)

Bicycle Shops

Bean's Bikes Inc., 10 West Lancaster Avenue, Paoli, PA (610-640-9910)

Bike Line, Paoli Shopping Center, Paoli, PA (610-647-8023)

Bike Line, 740 West DeKalb Pike, King of Prussia, PA (610-337-3003)

Metropolis Bicycles, 4159 Main Street, Manayunk (Philadelphia), PA (215 508-0350)

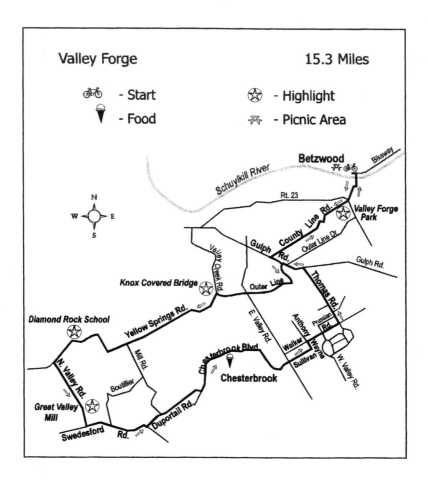

Valley Forge

15.3 Miles

🚲 - Start

🍦 - Food

✪ - Highlight

🏕 - Picnic Area

Central Montgomery Sampler

- 30 miles (31.75 miles with optional side trip to Skippack)
- Start and end at the Norristown Farm Park
- Terrain: rolling hills with a few steep climbs

Highlights

- Norristown Farm Park
- Evansburg State Park
- Olympic champion's horse farm
- Village of Skippack
- Accessible by rail from Philadelphia

Central Montgomery County is an area of contrast and paradox. Much of its rural character has been lost to suburban development. However, narrow corridors of beautiful hardwood forests and open fields still exist. At the eastern end of the ride, you can spot the tops of Philadelphia's highest skyscrapers from Upper Farm Road. In clear contrast, the western end of the ride is rural enough in character to boast a state park.

The ride begins at the Norristown Farm Park, the newest addition to the Montgomery County Park System. The farm once belonged to Norristown State Hospital, and raised food for the psychiatric patients at the facility. Many of the patients also worked on the farm as a form of therapy. Today, the park showcases 690 acres of woods and meadows, as well as a working farm.

At the 12.4 mile point of the ride is Vintage Farm, the home of Michael Matz. Matz, a long time member of the United States

Equestrian Team, won a silver medal in the 1996 Olympics. In addition to his equestrian achievements, Matz is credited with saving the lives of two children during a plane crash in Souix City, Iowa.

The optional trip into the village of Skippack is worth taking for the interesting array of shops and restaurants. The village enjoys a very fine reputation for antique stores as well as arts and crafts shops. While the village also contains many outstanding restaurants, most are a little too formal to visit in cycling attire. A delightful exception is Mal's American Diner, visible from the intersection of Route 73 and Store Road. Famous for its breakfast entrees, Mal's also has a fantastic lunch menu. The restaurant is a favorite destination for local bike clubs. Right next to Mal's is Skippack Bike and Blade, a small but friendly bicycle shop.

Another food stop option is Merrymead Farm, located just off the 23.8 mile mark. The excitement here centers on ice cream and other dairy treats. However, you can also find baked goods and fresh farm produce (in season). Live farm animals complete the ambiance of this lively dairy bar.

Getting to Norristown Farm Park

Norristown Farm Park is located on Germantown Pike, between Swede Street and Whitehall Road, just northwest of the borough of Norristown. Traveling west on Germantown Pike, the entrance is on the left, just opposite North Wales Road. There is a sign, but unfortunately it is well past the intersection. The best way to find the entrance is to look for the sign indicating North Wales Road. There is also a sign for Barley Sheaf Townhouses, which one passes before coming to the Farm Park.

Recently, SEPTA has allowed bicycles on its rail lines during off-peak hours. To access this ride using SEPTA, take the R6 to Norristown's Elm Street station (the last one on the line). As you get off the train, make a left turn and walk your bike up to Elm Street. Turning left, take Elm Street to Stanbridge Street. Make a right turn onto Stanbridge Street. Take Stanbridge Street to

Sterigere Street. At the traffic light, make a left turn onto Sterigere Street. Then make a right turn at the next traffic light onto Whitehall Road. Join the ride at the 1.25 mile mark, where the ride crosses the parking lot across from the Norristown High School.

The Ride

0.0	R	From the parking lot of the Montgomery County Farm Park Visitor's Center (facing the Visitor's Center), make a right turn onto the bike path that parallels Upper Farm Road. It is also possible to make a right turn onto Upper Farm Road, but the park officials would like you to use the bike path.
0.6	BR	Bear right onto Upper Farm Road.
0.65	BR	Cross a bridge and bear right back onto the bike path. (If you used Upper Farm Road, rejoin the bike path now.)
1.2	R	Turn right off the bike path into the parking lot across from Norristown High School.
1.25	S	Cross Whitehall Road onto Eagle Drive. Caution: busy road.
1.5	BR	Bear right, staying on Eagle Drive.
1.9	L	Turn left onto Burnside Ave.
2.5	R	At the Burnside/Oakland Park, turn right onto Oakland Road.
3.3	R	Turn right onto Trooper Road.
4.1	S	Straight, crossing Germantown Pike. Begin a steep ascent.
5.0	L	Turn left onto Woodland Avenue.

5.4	S	Straight, crossing Valley Forge Road. Caution: busy road.
5.6	L	Turn left onto Dell Road.
6.0	L	Turn left onto Quarry Hall Road.
6.2	R	Turn right onto Mill Road. Enjoy a pleasant descent!
7.7	R	Turn right onto Grange Avenue.
8.2	L	Turn left onto Water Street.
9.2	R	Turn right and walk your bicycle around the barricade, using the pedestrian bridge to cross Skippack Creek. Continue walking on the path on the other side of the creek.
9.3	S	Rejoin Mill Road straight ahead. The entrance to Evansburg State Park is just to the right. This road leads to picnic areas and a youth hostel.
10.0	L	Turn left onto Evansburg Road.
10.8	R	Turn right onto Township Line Road. You will soon pass Vintage Farm on the right.
11.8	R	Turn right onto Hildebeitel Road.
12.4	R	Turn right onto Mill Road.
12.7	L	Turn left onto Collegeville Road.
13.2	R	Turn right onto Landis Road. View airport just before turning.
13.3	L	Turn left onto Collegeville Road.
15.1	R	Turn right onto Hallman Avenue.
15.5	L	Turn left onto Evansburg Road.
15.9	S	At the traffic light go straight, crossing Route 73.
16.3	L	Turn left onto Township Line Road.
16.7	R	Turn right onto Store Road.

Optional side trip to village of Skippack: To get to Skippack, make a left turn onto Store

Road. Take Store Road .87 miles into the village. To rejoin the ride, simply turn around and go back to the intersection of Store and Township Line Roads. Go straight on Store Road.

18.9	R	Turn right onto Rittenhouse Road. View golf course on right.
19.3	R	Turn right onto Old Forty Foot Road.
19.7	L	Turn left onto Old Morris Road.
20.3	R	Turn right onto Springer Road.
20.9	L	Turn left onto Kriebel Road (Unmarked. Look for green and tan sign saying "Towamencin Trail").
21.2	S	Go straight at stop sign. Caution: busy road.
22.1	R	Turn right onto Trumbauer Road. Immediately cross a pretty stone bridge.
22.4	L	Turn left onto Morris Road.
23.3	S	Go straight at the traffic light, crossing Valley Forge Road. Make a right turn here to go to Merrymead Farm. Valley Forge Road is very busy and extreme caution needs to be taken in making the left turn into Merrymead. To rejoin the route, retrace Valley Forge Road to Morris Road, making a right turn onto Morris Road.
24.6	R	Turn right onto Berks Road.
25.9	S	Go straight, crossing route 73. Caution: busy road!
26.7	L	Turn left onto Bean Road. Use caution crossing railroad tracks just before North Wales Road.
27.8	R	Turn right onto North Wales Road.
28.6	S	Go straight crossing Township Line Road. A Wawa store is on the left.

29.5	S	Go straight, crossing Germantown Pike to enter the Norristown Farm Park.
29.8	R	Make a right turn onto Upper Farm Road.
30.0	END	End the ride at the Visitors Center of Norristown Farm Park.

FYI

Evansburg State Park, Collegeville (610-489-3729)
Mal's American Diner, Skippack (610-584-0900)
Merrymead Farm, Lansdale (610-584-4410)
Norristown Farm Park, Norristown (610-270-0215)

Bicycle Shops

Bike and Blade, 4002 Skippack Pike, Skippack, PA (610-222-0560)

Bikefit Inc., 1987 West Main Street, Jeffersonville, PA (610-539-8393)

Bikesport, 325 West Main Street, Trappe, PA (610-489-7300)

Bike Works, 500 Main Street, Harleysville, PA (215-513-7550)

Pedaller Bike Shop, 840 West Main Street, Lansdale, PA (215-361-2909)

Steve's Bike and Fitness, 1510 DeKalb Pike, Blue Bell, PA (610-275-4010)

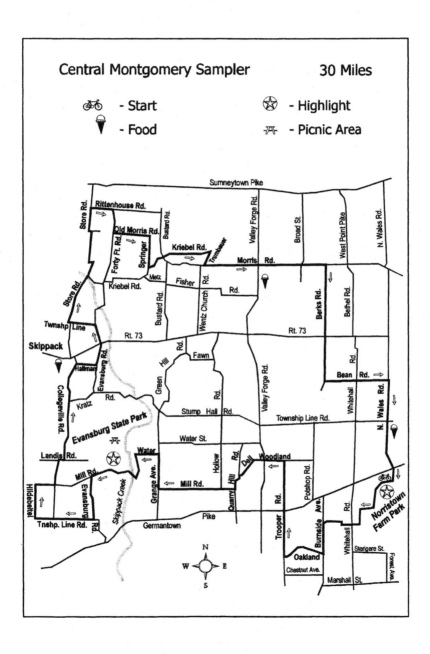

Two Outstanding Parks: Evansburg and Green Lane

- 42.1 Miles (43.85 miles with optional side trip to Skippack)
- Start and end at Evansburg State Park
- Terrain: Rolling hills with a few steep uphills

Highlights

- Evansburg State Park
- Eastern State Game Farm
- Green Lane Park
- Village of Skippack

Both Evansburg State Park and Green Lane County Park provide welcome respites from the congestion of urbanized living. The area between the two parks has not lost too much of its rural character and plenty of pretty roads for cycling still exist.

The ride begins inside Evansburg State Park, an area first settled by the Unami people of the Lenni Lenape Nation. The first European settlers were hearty Mennonites who farmed the region, beginning in the eighteenth century. Structures dating from this period still exist within the park, as well as in the surrounding countryside. These include the park Visitor Center, a Mennonite home from the early 1700's. Activities in the park include hiking on six miles of trails along Skippack Creek, and trout fishing.

The second park covered by the ride is the Green Lane County Park. Until very recently, this area contained two separate parks, the Upper Perkiomen Park and the Green Lane Reservoir Park. The two adjoining parks have now merged into one, making the Green Lane Park the largest in the Montgomery County system. The ride also passes through Sunrise Mill. This area was the site of a proposed county park. While the park itself has never developed, enough open space was preserved to create a beautiful natural environment.

As on the Central Montgomery Sampler ride, you can take a short side trip and visit Skippack. Please read the appropriate section in "Central Montgomery Sampler" to find out more about what this pretty little village has to offer.

The village of Green Lane, 24.4 miles into the ride, has both a grocery store and a convenience store for food purchases, as well as restaurants. Mal's American Diner in Skippack is also a great place to replenish the carbs. Picnic areas are located in both parks.

Getting to Evansburg State Park

From the Philadelphia area, take the Schuylkill Expressway or PA Turnpike to King of Prussia (Valley Forge turnpike exit), and then take Route 422 west to the Route 29 exit. Take Route 29 north to Collegeville. Make a right turn onto Main Street. Route 29 will bear left here, but you should continue straight on Main Street and cross the bridge. Then bear left onto Germantown Pike. Follow Germantown Pike for 1.25 miles, passing through the little town of Evansburg, and turn left onto Skippack Creek Road. Go one mile to the stop sign, turn left on Mill Road, and immediately turn right into the park entrance. The picnic area will be on the left, .7 miles from the entrance, and across from the Youth Hostel.

The Ride

0.0	L	Begin at the parking lot at Evansburg State Park's picnic area. Facing the Youth Hostel, make a left turn onto the access road leaving the park..
0.7	R	Make a right turn onto Mill Road.
1.3	R	Make a right turn onto Evansburg Road.
2.2	L	Make a left turn onto Miller Road.
2.6	L	Make a left turn onto Collegeville Road.
3.2	R	Make a right turn onto Landis Road.
3.7	L	Make a left turn onto Bridge Road (Route 113).
4.4	R	Make a right turn onto Perkiomen Creek Road. Caution: you will be riding downhill and the sign is hard to see.
5.8	L	Make a left turn onto Graterford Road. Graterford Prison is on the right. (Caution: watch for escaping convicts!)
6.1	S	Straight, crossing Route 29. Graterford Road becomes Bridge Street.
6.8	BL	Bear left, staying on Bridge Street.
7.9	R	Make a right turn onto Township Line Road.
8.4	L	Make a left turn onto Cemetery Road.
8.8	L	Make a left turn onto Limerick Road.
10.2	BL	Bear left onto Sunset Road.
10.9	R	Make a right turn onto Graterford Road.
11.4	BL	Bear slightly left onto North Limerick.
11.4	R	Immediately, make a quick right onto Metka Road.
12.5	R	Make a right turn onto State Game Farm Road.

13.8	L	Make a left turn onto Menj Road. The sign is on the left and hard to see.
14.8	L	Make a left turn onto Mine Hill Road. The sign is on the left and hard to see.
15.3	L	Make a left turn onto Yerger Road.
15.6	S	Go straight, staying on Yerger Road.
17.0	R	Make a right turn onto Neiffler Road (unmarked). This is the Sunrise Mill area.
19.0	L	Make a left turn at the T onto Route 73.
19.3	R	Make a right turn onto Perkiomenville Road.
22.1	L	Make a left turn at the T onto Deep Creek Road. Enter Green Lane Park.
23.2	R	Make a right turn onto Green Lane Road.
24.2	R	Make a right turn onto Hill Road.
24.5	R	Make a right turn onto Route 29.
24.6	BR	In the village of Green Lane, bear right onto Route 29 south.
24.7	L	Make a left turn onto Walnut Street (look for the Union National Bank on the left).
25.3	R	Make a right turn onto Upper Ridge Road.
25.8	R	Make a right turn onto Perkiomenville Road.
26.4	L	Make a very hard left onto Crusher Road. If you get to Route 29, you went too far.
26.6	S	Climb a challenging hill. Crusher Road becomes Perkiomenville Road.
28.2	R	Make a right turn onto Old Skippack Road. The next three miles are awesome. The road is level or slightly downhill. Nice views on either side.
31.0	S	Old Skippack Road becomes Salfordville Road.
31.5	L	After crossing a pretty stream, make a left turn onto Groffs Mill Road.

31.7	R	Make a right turn onto Old Skippack Road.
32.0	L	Make a left turn onto Landis Road (unmarked). This is the first left after turning onto Old Skippack Road.
32.5	S	Straight, crossing Route 113. Caution: busy road.
33.8	L	Make a left turn at the T onto Morris Road.
34.8	R	Make a right turn onto Store Road.
36.7	L	Make a left turn onto Township Line Road.

Optional side trip to village of Skippack: To visit Skippack continue on Store Road another .87 miles into the village. To rejoin the ride, turn around and go back to the intersection of Store and Township Line Roads. Make a right turn onto Township Line Road.

37.1	R	Make a right turn onto Forty Foot Road.
37.5	S	Straight, crossing Route 73. Forty Foot Road becomes Evansburg Road.
38.4	L	Make a left at the T onto Kratz Road.
38.9	R	Make a right turn onto Anders Road.
39.6	S	Straight. Anders Road becomes Evansburg Road.
40.7	L	Make a left turn onto Mill Road.
41.4	L	Make a left turn into Evansburg Park entrance. Caution: oncoming vehicles have a blind corner.
42.1	END	End at picnic area.

FYI

Evansburg State Park, Collegeville (610-489-3729)
Green Lane Park, Green Lane, PA. (215-234-4528)
Mal's American Diner, Skippack (610-584-0900)

Bicycle Shops

Bike and Blade, 4002 Skippack Pike, Skippack, PA (610-222-0560)

Bikesport, 325 West Main Street, Trappe, PA (610-489-7300).

Indian Valley Bike Works, 500 Main Street, Harleysville, PA (215-513-7550).

Tailwind Bicycle Shop, 160 Main Street, Schwenksville, PA (610-287-7870).

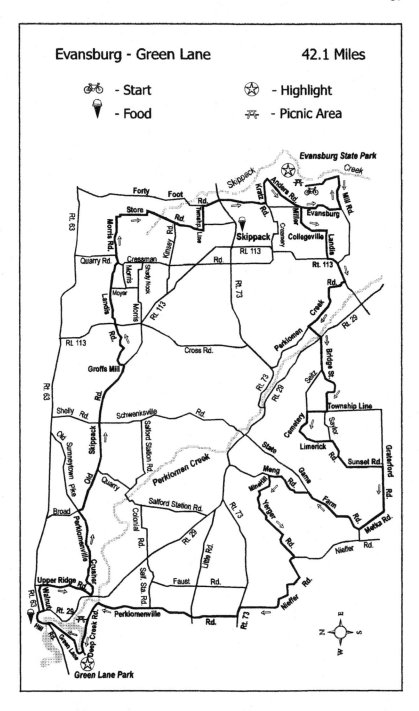

Evansburg - Green Lane

42.1 Miles

🚲 - Start

🍦 - Food

✪ - Highlight

🪑 - Picnic Area

Furnaces And Forges: Pottstown, Pine Forge And Colebrookdale

- 14.4 miles
- Start and end at Pottstown's Memorial Park
- Terrain: rolling with one steep climb

Highlights

- Memorial Park
- Beautiful Manatawny Creek
- Pine Forge Academy

The tri-county area just northwest of Pottstown played a significant role in the early iron industry of a very young nation. Pottstown itself was once proposed as the county seat, simply because it had a tavern and Norristown did not. John Potts, for whom the town is named, was a very wealthy ironmaster whose mansion is situated at the corner of King Street and Route 100. Pottsgrove Manor, as the mansion was called, is very close to the start of this ride and worth seeing if time permits.

After leaving Memorial Park, you ride parallel to the lovely Manatawny Creek to Pine Forge. Prior its conversion to a school in 1945, Pine Forge was one of many historical iron forges in the area. The forge also functioned as a stop on the Underground Railroad just before the Civil War. The nationally renowned Pine Forge Academy Choir practices in a building that was originally the stable for the old forge.

Before winding back to Pottstown, you pay a visit to the picturesque village of Colebrookdale, once the home of Colebrookdale Furnace. Built in 1720, Colebrookdale Furnace is probably the first blast furnace to operate in Pennsylvania. The furnace was named after the Colebrook Furnace in England.

Two restaurants, The Greshville Inn and the Little Oley Tavern, are noted along the route. Both offer tavern fare, including sandwiches. Also there is a lovely little creek-side picnic area on Manatawny Street between Pottstown and Pine Forge. The Ice House Deli, located on Manatawny Street near the beginning of the ride, is a another good source of food.

Getting to Pottstown's Memorial Park

From the Philadelphia area, take Route 422 west to Pottstown. Exit Route 422 at Hanover Street, taking Hanover Street into the center of town. Turn left onto King Street. Follow King Street to Manatawny Street, making a left turn onto Manatawny. Memorial Park is on the left of Manatawny Street, with a parking lot close to the Vietnam Veterans Memorial area. Additional parking can be found on side streets, as well as at the Gruber Swimming Pool, just off the King Street entrance to the park.

The Ride

0.0	L	From the Memorial Park parking lot on Manatawny Street, make a left turn onto Manatawny Street.
2.4	S	Caution: Cross railroad tracks at right angle to the tracks.
3.2	L	Make a left turn at the T onto Pine Forge Road (unmarked). Signs will point to Pine Forge and Greshville. Pine Forge Academy is about half a mile up the road.

4.1	R	Make a right turn onto Douglas Drive.
7.5	R	Make a right turn onto Route 562.
7.9	R	Make a right turn onto Greshville Road (sign on the left). This is the first right turn after turning onto Route 562. The Greshville Inn is on the left on Route 562.
8.7	S	Caution: railroad tracks at the bottom of the hill.
8.75	BL	Bear left, staying on Greshville Road.
9.0	R	Make a right turn onto Farmington Avenue, entering the little town of Colebrookdale.
9.2	BR	Bear right onto Colebrookdale Road. The Little Oley Tavern is on the right. Ascend a very short, steep hill followed by a long, not quite uninterrupted descent. Caution: stop sign at bottom of the hill, just before Manatawny Street.
12.0	L	Make a left turn onto Manatawny Street.
14.4	END	End ride at the parking lot for Memorial Park on Manatawny Street.

FYI

The Greshville Inn, Boyertown (610-367-6994)
Ice House Deli, Pottstown (610-326-9999)
Little Oley Tavern, Boyertown (610-367-2353)
Pottsgrove Manor, Pottstown (610-326-4014)

Bicycle Shop

Bike Line, 1386 N. State Street, Pottstown, PA (610-326-0780)

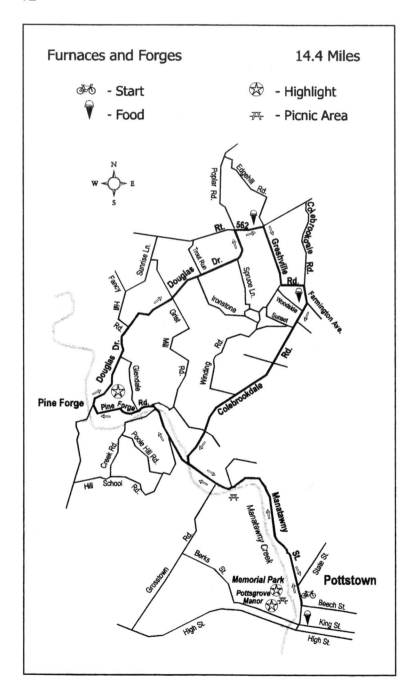

Furnaces and Forges   14.4 Miles

- Start
- Food
- Highlight
- Picnic Area

Woodcutters, Ironmasters and Moulders: Hopewell Furnace And French Creek

- 14.0 miles (14.8 miles with optional side trip to Hopewell Lake)
- Start and end at Hopewell Furnace National Historic Site
- Terrain: hilly

Highlights

- Hopewell Furnace National Historic Site
- French Creek State Park
- Interesting collection of railroad equipment

During the late 18th century, southeastern Berks County was home to many of the finest charcoal-fueled iron furnaces in the nation. However, by the mid 19th century, newer methods of producing iron were discovered and most of the furnaces disappeared. In 1938, the National Park Service restored the old Hopewell Furnace and began administering the area as a National Historic Site. Today, the restored furnace, waterwheel, blast machinery, ironmaster's mansion and other miscellaneous structures remind visitors of a thriving industry that once flourished in this unique part of Pennsylvania.

Almost surrounding Hopewell Furnace is French Creek State Park. When Hopewell was in operation, the area now occupied by the park produced the charcoal necessary to fuel the large blast furnace. While woodcutters chopped the trees, colliers burned the wood in hearths to produce the needed charcoal. Today, the park supports a diverse ecosystem, while providing outdoor recreation opportunities to the ever expanding population of southeastern Pennsylvania. Activities that can be enjoyed in the Park include hiking, camping, swimming, fishing, boating, orienteering and disc golf (sometimes known as "Frisbee golf"). The area is especially beautiful in autumn.

A grocery store is located at the 8 mile mark of the ride, however it is closed on Sundays. The Scott's Run and Hopewell Lake areas are scenic spots for eating a carry-along lunch.

If you wish to do a longer ride, it should be noted that this ride can easily be combined with the St. Peters and Hopewell Village ride. After completing the loop, pick up the St. Peters ride by making a right turn from Route 345 onto Hopewell Road instead of turning left into the driveway for Hopewell Village. This is the 7.4 mile mark of the St. Peters ride.

Getting to Hopewell Furnace National Historic Site

From the Philadelphia area, take the Pennsylvania Turnpike to the Route 100-Downingtown Interchange. After leaving the turnpike, take Route 100 north to Route 23. Make a left turn onto Route 23 west. Make a right turn onto Route 345 north. Hopewell Furnace is on the left, about a mile and a half past the south entrance of French Creek State Park.

The Ride

0.0	S	Begin in the parking lot of Hopewell Furnace National Historic Center, just opposite the visitors' center. Ride out the driveway (called Mark Bird Lane). For a fee, you can pick apples in season in the orchard surrounding the parking lot.
0.3	R	Make a right turn onto Route 345 south.

1.7	R	Make a right turn and enter French Creek State Park on South Entrance Road (brown sign says "French Creek State Park").
2.9	L	Make a left turn onto Park Road

Optional Side Trip to Hopewell Lake: To get to Hopewell Lake, make a right turn onto Park Road. Follow Park Road .4 mile to the Lake. To rejoin ride, simply turn around and ride back to the intersection of South Entrance Road and Park Road. Continue straight on Park Road at this intersection.

5.4	R	Make a right turn onto Kline Road.
6.0	R	Make a right turn onto Red Hill Road.
6.4	L	Make a left turn at the T onto Cold Run Road (unmarked). Enjoy a nice downhill cruise.
7.8	R	Make a right turn onto Route 82, into the tiny village of Geigertown.
8.0	R	Make a right turn onto Geigertown Road. After making the turn, Shirey's Groceries is on the right. An interesting collection of old railroad equipment can be seen on the left.
8.7	R	Make a right turn onto Kratz Road. This road and the next one contain steep climbs.
9.6	L	Make a left turn onto Fire Tower Road.
10.0	S	Reenter French Creek State Park.
10.1	BL	Bear left. A right turn will take you up to the fire tower. It would be worth the climb if the tower were open, but unfortunately, it is closed to the public. There is still a picnic area there, with grills and a fireplace.
10.8	BR	Bear right at sign pointing towards Main Park Area, Scott's Run Lake, and Campground. Scott's Run Lake itself is on a marked one-way side road on the right and is worth visiting.

11.8	L	Make a left turn at the T onto Park Road (unmarked, but there is a sign pointing to Route 345.)
12.9	R	Make a right turn onto Route 345.
13.5	R	Make a right turn onto Mark Bird Drive, entering Hopewell Furnace National Historic Site.
14.0	END	End ride in parking lot opposite visitors' center.

FYI

French Creek State Park, Elverson (610-582-9680)
Hopewell Furnace National Historical Site, Elverson (610-582-8773)
Shirey's Groceries, Birdsboro (610-286-9835)

Bicycle Shops

Bike Line, 1386 N. State Street, Pottstown, PA (610-326-0780)

Lebo's Pedal Parlor, 2200 Penn Ave., West Lawn, PA (610)-678-3191)

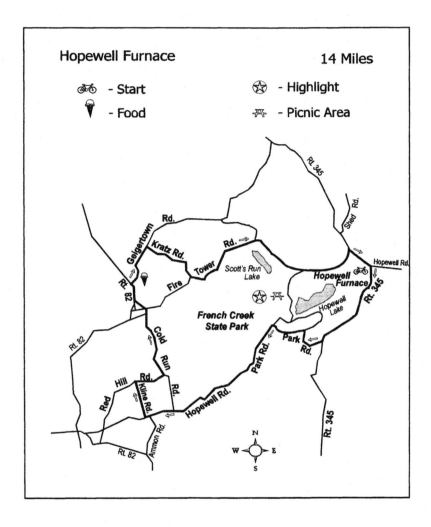

Hopewell Furnace   14 Miles

🚲 - Start   ✪ - Highlight

🍦 - Food   🪑 - Picnic Area

A Portrait Of Two Villages:
St. Peters And Hopewell

- 10.7 miles (11.3 miles with optional trip to Hopewell Village)
- Start and finish at St. Peters Village
- Terrain: rolling with a few steep climbs

Highlights

- St. Peters Village
- Beautiful horse farms
- Hopewell Furnace National Historic Site

St. Peters Village is one of many quaint little arts and crafts centers located in the western ends of the suburban counties. At the south end of the one-street town is a handsome Victorian inn that features fine dining in a lovely setting. Walking north, you can easily find an interesting variety of stores selling anything from antiques to fudge. While researching this ride, we talked with the shopkeeper at the fudge store and found out that bicycle enthusiasts come from as far away as Harrisburg to enjoy this interesting part of the state. Behind the shops is a beautiful glen, highlighted by a fast-running boulder-filled creek.

At the other end of the ride is Hopewell Furnace National Historic Site. Operated by the federal government, the site is a restored early 19th century iron making village and includes a furnace, waterwheel, ironmaster's mansion and other buildings.

If you wish to take a longer ride, it should be noted that this route can easily be combined with the Hopewell Furnace and French Creek ride. At the 6 mile mark in the ride, look for a road and sign on the left for French Creek State Park. Turn left into the park here, joining the Hopewell Furnace and French Creek Ride at the 1.7 mile mark.

Food is available at a number of snack bars in St. Peters Village.

Getting to St. Peters Village

From the Philadelphia area, take Route 422 west to Route 100 south (just south of Pottstown). Continue on Route 100 south to Route 23 west. After passing through Coventryville, start looking for a sign pointing to St. Peters Village on the right. Warwick County Park will be on the left. Turn onto St. Peters Road at the sign to get to the village. The parking lot from which the ride starts is at the opposite end of the village.

The Ride

0.0	R	From the south end of the St. Peters Village parking lot (next to Rosie's Café), make a right turn onto St. Peters Road, passing through the village.
0.6	R	Make a right turn onto Route 23. This is a busy road, but it has a nice shoulder.
2.0	R	Make a right turn onto Trythall Road. The sign is impossible to see, but there is a prominent green and white sign for Warwick Woods Campgrounds just before the road.
3.5	L	Make a left turn onto Harmonyville Road.
3.7	BL	Bear left, staying on Harmonyville Road.

4.5	BL	Bear left, staying on Harmonyville Road. Travel through State Game Lands.
5.4	R	Make a right turn onto Pine Swamp Road (Route 345).
7.4	R	Make a right turn onto Hopewell Road.
9.3	R	Make a right turn onto Keim Road. Pass pretty horse farm on the left.
9.5	L	Make a left turn onto Harmonyville Road. The sign says "Bradley's Corner."
9.9	R	Make a right turn onto St. Peters Road.
10.7	END	End the ride at the St. Peters Village parking lot

FYI

French Creek State Park, Elverson (610-582-9680)
Hopewell Furnace National Historical Site, Elverson (610-582-8773)
St. Peters Inn, St. Peters (610-469-3809)

Bicycle Shops

Bike Line, 1386 N. State Street, Pottstown, PA (610-326-0780)

Lebo's Pedal Parlor, 2200 Penn Ave., West Lawn, PA (610-678-3191

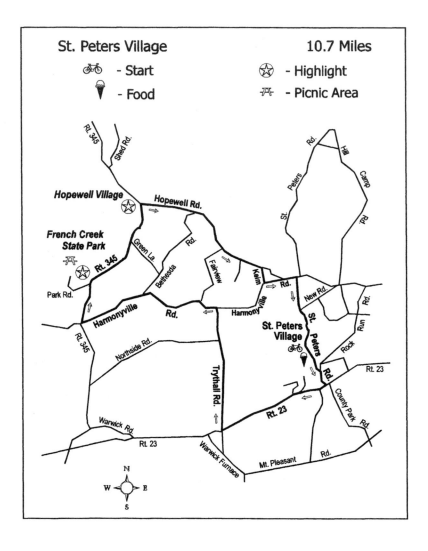

St. Peters Village — 10.7 Miles

🚲 - Start   ⊛ - Highlight
🍦 - Food   ⛱ - Picnic Area

The "Mountains" Of Montgomery County: Pennypacker Mills And Spring Mount

- 16.3 miles
- Start and end at historic Pennypacker Mills
- Terrain: hilly

Highlights

- Pennypacker Mills Mansion
- Spring Mountain Ski Area
- Bergey's Mill Farmstead

Except for the Hawk Mountain region, there is no area within southeastern Pennsylvania that is truly mountainous. However, the hills surrounding the Schwenksville-Spring Mount Area contain just enough vertical drop to justify a ski area. Spring Mountain never claims to compete in the same market as Aspen. Yet its close proximity to Philadelphia and its western suburbs has earned the little enterprise a loyal following.

For the cyclist, the climb over Spring Mountain certainly is not Le'Alpe d"Huez. But this climb, as well as others along the route, will make for a vigorous ride.

The ride begins at Pennypacker Mills, a historical site preserved by the Montgomery County Department of History and Cultural Arts. The mansion on the property was home to Samuel W. Pennypacker, a distinguished lawyer, historian, farmer and

Governor of Pennsylvania. From February, 1901 to May, 1902, renovations were made to transform what was then a stone German farmhouse into a colonial mansion. In 1985, four years after its purchase, the county opened the house and grounds to the public. The county sponsors numerous special events on the property throughout the year, including watercolor painting workshops, an Earth Day Celebration, and natural heritage walks.

The ride also passes another historical home, the Bergey Mill Farmstead, at the 12.7 mile mark. Tours are available by appointment.

Although the ride contains two taverns, there are no lunch stops on the route. Restaurants and grocery stores are located in Schwenksville, near the start of the ride. If you would like to carry a lunch, there is a lovely picnic area just before crossing the bridge at 10.6 miles on Camp WaWa Road.

Getting to Pennypacker Mills

From Philadelphia's northwestern suburbs, take Route 73 west through Blue Bell, Center Point and Skippack. Just before coming to the bridge over the Perkiomen Creek and the intersection with Route 29, turn right onto Haldeman Road and an immediate left into Pennypacker Mills.

The Ride

0.0	S	Begin the ride at the parking lot of Pennypacker Mills Mansion. Ride out the driveway back towards Haldeman Road. (The driveway is a dirt road, but very well maintained).
0.3	L	Make a sharp left turn onto Haldeman Road. Pass the Perkiomen Valley Watershed Association on the right. View the mansion on the left.

0.7	L	Make a left turn onto Dieber Road.
1.0	L	Make a left turn onto Pennypacker Road. There is a brief, but pretty view of Schwenksville on the left.
1.4	R	Make a right turn at the stop sign onto Schwenksville Road (unmarked).
2.1	BL	Bear left, staying on Schwenksville Road.
2.5	L	Make a left turn onto Spring Mount Road. Look for sign for Spring Mountain Ski Area. Pass the ski area on the left.
3.3	R	Inside the village of Spring Mount, make a right turn onto Main Street. Joe's Spring Mt. Hotel is on the right.
3.7	S	Continue straight at stop sign.
4.1	R	Make a right turn onto Schwenk Road.
4.8	R	Make a right turn at the T onto Salford Station Road (unmarked).
6.3	S	Entering the tiny town of Salford, go straight. Salford Station Road becomes Salford Street.
6.4	S	Continue straight on Salford Street (Salford Post Office is on the right).
7.5	R	Make a right turn onto Old Skippack Road. Pass through the little town of Salfordville, with pretty views on both sides of the road.
9.6	BR	Bear right. Old Skippack Road becomes Salford-ville Road.
10.3	R	Make a right turn onto Camp WaWa Road.
10.6	S	Cross an iron bridge. Caution: If you have never crossed an iron bridge before, it can be a strange feeling, especially on racing tires. The bridge can be very slippery if wet. There is a pretty picnic area on the right, just before the bridge.

11.5	L	Make a left turn onto Haldeman Road.
12.2	S	Keep going straight. Haldeman Road becomes Bergey Mill Road.
12.7	S	Pass the Bergey Mill Farmstead on the left.
13.1	R	Make a right turn onto Cross Road.
14.4	R	Make a right turn onto Route 73. Caution: Route 73 is very busy, but has a wide shoulder.
16.0	R	Make a right turn onto Haldeman Road and an immediate left turn into Pennypacker Mills.
16.3	END	End the ride in the parking lot of the mansion.

FYI

Bergey Mill Farmstead, Schwenksville (610-287-6010)
Pennypacker Mills, Schwenksville (610-287-9349)

Bicycle Shops

Bikesport, 325 Main Street, Trappe, PA (610-489-7300)

Indian Valley Bike Works, 500 Main Street, Harleysville, PA (215-513-7550)

Tailwind Bicycle Shop, 160 Main Street, Schwenksville, PA (610-287-7870)

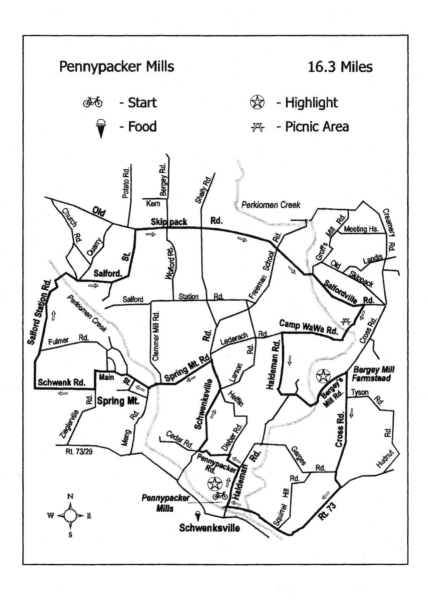

Pennypacker Mills   16.3 Miles

- Start   - Highlight

- Food   - Picnic Area

Deep Creek And The Upper Perkiomen Valley

- 10.1 miles
- Start and end at the Deep Creek Lake area of Green Lane Park
- Terrain: hilly

Highlights

- Green Lane Park
- Upper Montgomery County farm country
- Beautiful Deep Creek Lake

Recently, the Upper Perkiomen Valley and Green Lane Reservoir Parks merged to form the Green Lane Park, the largest in the Montgomery County System. The original Upper Perkiomen Valley section of this popular recreation area was founded in 1939 on 425 acres of land purchased by the county. When the Green Lane Reservoir section was added, the park reached it's present size of approximately 3200 acres. Activities at the park include canoeing and boating on Deep Creek Lake, hiking, and picnicking. Concerts are sometimes held in the summer, and in winter the park is popular for sledding, cross country skiing, and ice skating.

The ride visits the tiny village of Perkiomenville, famous at the turn of the century for a rather large cattle auction which took place behind the present day Perkiomenville Hotel. According to historians, cattle were brought in by railroad from as far away as Ohio for the auction. The ride also visits the Deep Creek Valley, which played a significant part in the early industrial development of the area. However, today very little evidence exists of industry. Much of the valley is either woodlands or home lots.

Food is not available along the route. However, Green Lane Park is a wonderful place for a picnic before or after the ride. Lakeside picnic tables and grills are available there. There are also restaurants located in Green Lane, not far from the start of the ride.

Getting to Green Lane Park

Traveling north on Route 29, there are signs for Green Lane Park on the left hand side of the road, just before entering the Borough of Green Lane. Cross the bridge after turning left from Route 29. The parking lot at Snyder and Deep Creek Roads is just a little beyond the guard house. Green Lane Park is also accessible from Route 63. Going east on Route 63, go through the Borough of Green Lane. While still inside the borough, turn left onto Route 29 and follow the directions above.

The Ride

0.0	R	From the parking lot at the corner of Snyder and Deep Creek Roads, make a right turn onto Deep Creek Road.
0.5	R	Inside the little village of Perkiomenville, make a right turn onto Perkiomenville Road.
2.4	R	Make a right turn onto Little Road (marked by sign on left). Little Road runs along the top of a ridge with nice views of the valley on the left.
3.6	R	Make a right turn onto Township Line Road
3.7	L	Make a left turn onto Little Road (unmarked). It is the first left turn after turning onto Township Line Road.

5.0	BL	Bear left, staying on Little Road.
5.1	R	Make a right turn, staying on Little Road.
5.8	R	Make a right turn onto Schultz Road. If you come to a stop sign, you are at Route 663. Go back to Schultz Road. You went too far!
6.65	S	Go straight. Schultz Road becomes Deep Creek Road.
7.35	S	Go straight at the stop sign, staying on Deep Creek Road. Caution: stop sign is at the bottom of a short, but steep hill and opposing traffic does not stop.
9.5	S	Go straight at the stop sign, staying on Deep Creek Road.
10.1	END	End the ride at the parking lot on the corner of Snyder and Deep Creek Roads.

FYI

Green Lane Park, Green Lane, PA. (215-234-4528)

Bicycle Shops

Bike Line, Route 202 & 309 & 463, Montgomeryville, PA (215-361-7900)

Indian Valley Bike Works, 500 Main Harleysville, PA (215-256-6613)

Tailwind Bike Shop Ltd., 351 Main Street, Pennsburg, PA (215-541-4949)

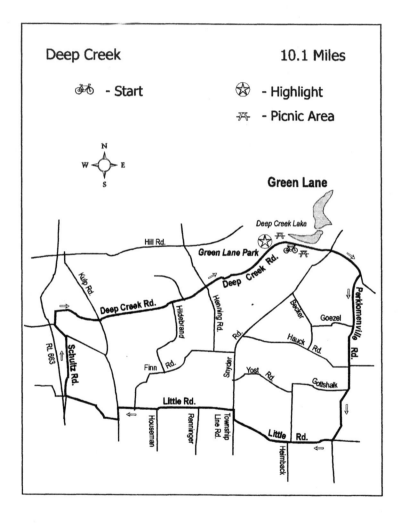

A Little Gem Of A Ride: Unami Creek

- 9.6 miles
- Start and finish at Unami Creek Park in Sumneytown
- Terrain: rolling, with one long, difficult climb at the start

Highlights

- Unami Creek
- Thick forests

Just north of the Upper Perkiomen lies a fast running, boulder strewn stream called Unami Creek. Next to the creek runs Swamp Creek Road. However, the terrain is anything but swampy. The creek speeds down a hillside, occasionally interrupted by small dams. The ride is a little tough as it moves out of the valley, using roads just west of Unami Creek. However, no hard work goes unrewarded. The last four to five miles of the ride cruise gradually downhill through woods and along the beautiful creek.

The road next to the creek may be busy during the first couple weekends of fishing season. Early in the fishing season may not be the best time to do the ride, unless both fishing and cycling are on the agenda! The ride is especially pretty a little later, in May, when dogwood trees and wildflowers bloom along the road.

There are not any places to purchase food along the route. Your best bet is to bring a picnic lunch to enjoy at one of the many scenic spots beside the creek! Food is also available in Sumneytown, near the start of the ride.

Getting to the Unami Creek Park in Sumneytown

The Unami Creek Park in Sumneytown, located on Swamp Creek Road, is quite easy to find. From the Kulpsville or Harleysville area, travel west on Route 63 until you get to Sumneytown. Within the village of Sumneytown, make a right turn onto Geryville Pike. Very shortly thereafter, make a right turn onto Swamp Creek Road. The park is at the intersection of Swamp Creek Road and Geryville Pike.

The Ride

0.0	L	Standing in the park, facing Swamp Creek Road, make a left turn onto Swamp Creek Road.
0.1	R	Make a right turn onto Geryville Pike. Ascend a mile long hill, which is the only difficult climb on the ride.
1.0	R	Make a right turn onto Upper Ridge Road. Pass the Delmont-Hart Scout Reservation.
4.2	R	Make a right turn, staying on Upper Ridge Road.
4.9	R	Make a right turn onto Swamp Creek Road. Nice scenery ahead!
6.1	L	Make a left turn, staying on Swamp Creek Road. Cross a stone bridge over Swamp Creek.
6.3	BR	Bear right, staying on Swamp Creek Road.
9.35	L	After crossing another pretty stone bridge, turn left, staying on Swamp Creek Road.
9.6	END	End back at Unami Creek Park on the left.

Bicycle Shops

Adventure Bicycle Company, 1625 Hatfield Valley Road, Hatfield, PA (215-368-8383)

Indian Valley Bike Works, 500 Main Street, Harleysville, PA (215-513-7550)

Scooter's Bike Shop, 130 N. Main Street, Souderton, PA (215-723-5909)

Tailwind Bike Shop Ltd., 351 Main Street, Pennsburg, PA (215-541-4949)

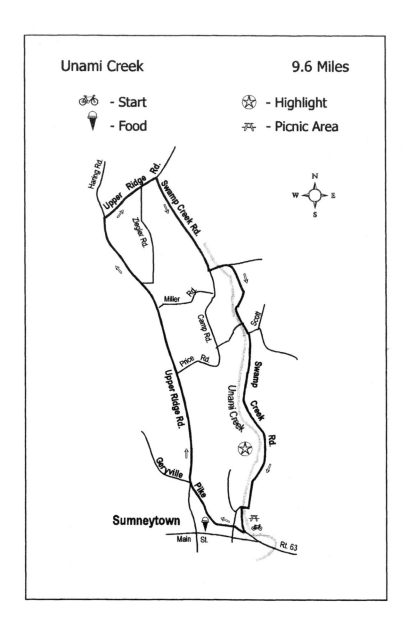

Unami Creek

9.6 Miles

- Start
- Highlight
- Food
- Picnic Area

The Chocoholic Ride:
Red Hill And Trumbauersville

- 19.9 miles
- Start and finish at the Green Lane Reservoir area of Green Lane Park (just outside Red Hill)
- Terrain: hilly

Highlights

- Green Lane Park
- Ann Hemyng Chocolate Factory
- Rural Montgomery and Bucks County countryside

The rolling hills along the border of Montgomery and Bucks Counties are home to more than just farms, forests, and scenic rural vistas. Tourists seldom find their way to little Trumbauersville, but those who do are rewarded with the opportunity to visit one of the best chocolate factories to be found anywhere. Ann Hemyng Candy, Inc. began in 1984 in Peddler's Village, a more well known Bucks County destination. In 1988 the company moved to Trumbauersville, where local demand resulted in the opening of a factory store. Chocolate is available here in all shapes and sizes. A wide assortment of other candies are also sold, and tours of the factory can be arranged for small groups. The factory closes in summer, but the store remains open.

The ride begins in Red Hill at the Green Lane Reservoir section of Green Lane Park. This large county park is popular for boating and fishing, and has picnic tables and grills available. Red

Hill is a busy town with a number of stores and restaurants, but the ride quickly heads into more rural surroundings.

Food (other than chocolate) is available on the ride at Spor's General Store, located at the 9.2 mile mark. In addition to groceries and soft ice cream, a dining section is located in the back of Spor's, serving breakfast and lunch. The Finland Inn at the 12.7 mile mark serves lunch and dinner in an elegant atmosphere. For a meal before or after the ride, the Apple Dumpling Diner on Main Street in Red Hill is a popular destination.

This ride can be combined with the Unami Creek ride. From Upper Ridge Road, make a left turn onto Swamp Creek Road. Follow the directions for the Unami Creek ride, rejoining the Chocoholic Ride by making a left turn onto Finland Road from Upper Ridge Road. Remember that while this detour adds a beautiful downhill cruise along Unami Creek, it also includes a tough climb on Geryville Pike.

Getting to Green Lane Park in Red Hill

From the Philadelphia area, take the Pennsylvania Turnpike or Schuylkill Expressway to King of Prussia, and take Route 422 west to the Collegeville/Phoenixville exit. From the exit, take Route 29 north to Red Hill. Just at the border between Red Hill and Pennsburg, turn left onto 11th Street and follow it for .5 miles. The entrance to Green Lane Park (Walt Road Boat Launch Site) is on the right.

The Ride

| 0.0 | S | Begin at the small ranger station in the park, with the ranger station on your right and ride straight out the driveway. |
| 0.7 | R | Make a right turn onto Main Street. Caution: very busy street. |

0.7	L	Make an immediate left turn onto 11th Street (unmarked). You may want to walk your bicycle across Main Street because of traffic.

0.7   L   Make an immediate left turn onto 11th Street (unmarked). You may want to walk your bicycle across Main Street because of traffic.

1.3   L   Make a left turn onto St. Paul's Church Road.

1.5   L   Make a left turn onto Frye Road.

2.2   R   Make a right turn onto Buck Road.

4.3   R   Make a right turn at the T onto Old Plains Road (unmarked).

4.8   L   Make a left turn at stop sign onto Fennel Road.

6.2   S   At intersection with Canary Road, continue straight on Fennel Road.

6.3   R   Make a right turn at the T onto Kumry Road (unmarked). Caution: there is a short, steep downhill right before the turn.

8.6   S   Go straight at stop sign onto Allentown Road. You are now in the town of Trumbauersville.

9.0   S   Ann Hemyng Chocolate Factory is on the right.

9.3   R   Make a right turn onto West Broad Street (becomes Trumbauersville Road). Spor's General Store is on the left.

12.6   S   Go straight, staying on Trumbauersville Road. An optical illusion makes it look like the sign post is indicating that Trumbauersville Road bears to the right.

12.9   R   Make a right turn at the T in Finland onto Upper Ridge Road. (The sign says Finland Road). The Finland Inn is on the right. Upper Ridge Road climbs, sometimes steeply, for almost a mile.

13.8   BL   Bear left at stop sign, staying on Upper Ridge.

13.9   R   Make a right turn onto Finland Road and enjoy a downhill cruise.

15.5   BL   Bear left, staying on Finland Road.

15.8	L	Make a left turn at the T onto Geryville Pike (unmarked). Caution: you are going downhill when approaching this turn.
16.5	R	Make a right turn onto West Hendricks Road.
17.2	R	Make a right turn, staying on Hendricks Road.
17.75	R	Make a right turn onto 4th Street.
17.8	L	Make an immediate left turn onto Adams Street.
18.0	R	Make a right turn onto 6th Street.
18.3	L	Make a left turn onto James Road.
18.6	L	Make a left turn onto 11th Street.
19.2	R	Make a right turn onto Main Street. Watch out for the traffic.
19.2	L	Make an immediate left turn onto 11th Street. You may want to walk your bicycle across Main Street due to heavy traffic.
19.7	R	Make a right turn into Green Lane Park.
19.9	END	End at ranger station.

FYI

Ann Hemyng Candy, Inc., Trumbauersville (215-536-7004)
Apple Dumpling Diner, Red Hill (215-679-5000)
Finland Inn, Finland (215-679-0828)
Green Lane Park, Green Lane (215-234-4863)
Spor's General Store, Trumbauersville (215-536-6754)

Bicycle Shops

Cycledrome, 38 South 8th Street, Quakertown, PA (215-536-3443)

Tailwind Bike Shop Ltd., 351 Main Street, Pennsburg, PA (215-541-4949)

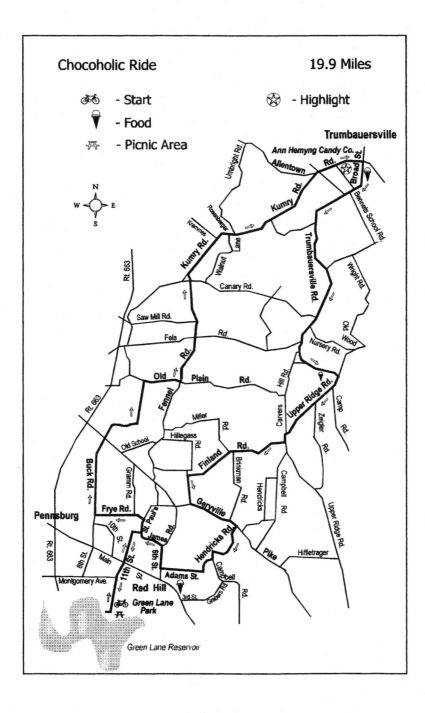

Chocoholic Ride   19.9 Miles

🚲 - Start   ✪ - Highlight

🍦 - Food

🪑 - Picnic Area

The Sheard's Mill Covered Bridge is one of many historic bridges in upper Bucks County.

The Less Visited Bucks County

- 21.8 miles
- Start and finish at Lake Towhee Park
- Terrain: rolling

Highlights

- Lake Towhee Park
- Sheard's Mill Covered Bridge
- Nockamixon Lake State Park Environmental Study Area
- Thayer Weed Farm

The area just east of Quakertown and Sellersville is the area most easily missed by the tourists speeding off to Doylestown and New Hope. Often named "The Great Swamp" on early maps, this route contains some interesting wetlands that are a favorite destination for bird watchers. Also along the route are two lakes, Towhee and Nockamixon, which are prime destinations for boaters, picnickers and fishing enthusiasts. The farms are not quite as well manicured as those between New Hope and Doylestown, but are quite charming in their own right and give the area a truly rural flavor. The many hardwood forests along the route make it one of our favorite rides for viewing fall foliage.

On the right at 1.2 miles, you will see the Parkway Restaurant . Reminiscent of a classic 1950's style drive-in, the Parkway serves shakes, burgers, fries, etc. On numerous weekends through the warm weather, the Parkway hosts classic car shows worth stopping to see.

At 3.2 miles, you will pass the Weisel Youth Hostel, the first county-operated hostel in the country, on the left. Very shortly afterward, you will see some rather interesting pyramids on the right.

Last, but not least, pass the Thayer Weed Farm at 12.7 miles. The sign on the right is small and easy to miss.

Getting to Lake Towhee Park

Lake Towhee, operated by the County of Bucks, is located on Old Bethlehem Road (not to be confused with Old Bethlehem Pike on our cue sheet) between Route 563 and the tiny village of Applebachsville. Take Route 611 north to the Route 313 exit in Doylestown. Travel west on Route 313. At the intersection of Routes 313 and 563, go north on Route 563. After passing the Nockamixon Lake Environmental Study Center, start looking for Old Bethlehem Road on the left. Once the turn onto Old Bethlehem Road is made, Lake Towhee Park is on the right. The sign is a little hard to see while traveling in this direction. If you enter the village of Applebachsville, you went just a bit too far.

The Ride

0.0	L	At the entrance to Lake Towhee Park, make a left turn onto Old Bethlehem Road
1.2	R	Make a right turn onto West Thatcher Road. The Parkway is on the corner.
1.7	L	Make a left turn onto Covered Bridge Road. .3 miles later, go through the Sheard's Mill Covered Bridge. The Tohicken Campground is on the left, just after the bridge.
2.55	L	Make a left turn at the T onto Richlandtown Road (unmarked).
3.8	L	Make a left turn onto Sterner Mill Road

3.85	R	Make a right turn onto Route 563 (unmarked). This road can be busy, but it has a nice shoulder. Immediately pass Nockamixon Lake State Park Environmental Study Area on left.
4.8	L	Make a left turn onto Route 313. Use caution. This is a busy intersection.
5.0	R	Make a right turn onto West Rock Road. It is the first right turn after entering Route 313. We do not want you to miss it. Route 313 is not fun to ride on.
6.5	R	After descending a short hill (pretty pond on left), make a right turn at the T onto Three Mile Run Road (unmarked).
8.6	R	Make a right turn onto Park Avenue. This becomes Old Bethlehem Pike (not to be confused with Old Bethlehem Road).
11.1	R	Make a right turn onto Paletown Road. Just before Paletown Road, you will see BARC Production Services on the left. Paletown Road is easy to miss, as you are gaining speed down a short hill.
12.1	R	Make a right turn onto Smoketown Road. The Commonwealth Flag Company is on the left. Smoketown Road becomes Muskrat Road. Pass the Thayer Weed Farm on the right at 12.7 miles.
13.1	L	Make a left turn onto Rich Hill Road, just after passing the state game lands on the left. This road becomes Rock Hill Road.
15.4	S	Cross Route 313. This is a busy intersection. Rock Hill Road becomes Ax Handle Road.
15.8	BL	Bear left, staying on Ax Handle Road.
16.6	R	Make a right turn onto Thatcher Road, immediately crossing a bridge over Morgan Creek.

17.8	L	Make a left turn onto Union Road. A signpost on the right will say "Richlandtown Road'" while a signpost on the left will say "Union Road."
18.65	R	Make a right turn onto Apple Road
19.4	R	Make a right turn onto Woodland Drive. You will see a sign straight ahead saying "Beck Road." After making the turn you should see a sign saying "Haycock Twp."
19.9	BL	Bear left onto Creamery Road.
20.2	BL	Bear left. Creamery Road becomes Apple Road, even later becoming Applebachsville Road.
21.35	R	Inside the tiny village of Applebachsville, make a right turn onto Old Bethlehem Road.
21.8	END	End at Lake Towhee Park on the left.

FYI

Lake Towhee Park, Applebachsville (215-757-0571)
Parkway Drive In Restaurant, Quakertown (215-538-2904)

Bicycle Shops

Bike Line, Main & Old Dublin, Doylestown, PA (215-348-8015)

Cycledrome, 38 South 8th Street, Quakertown, PA (215-536-3443)

Cycle Sports LTD., 641 North Main Street, Doylestown, PA (215-340-2526)

Freeman's Bicycle Shop, Routes 412 & 563, Ottsville, PA (610-847-5506)

Nestor's Sporting Goods, 99 N. West End Blvd., Quakertown, PA (215-529-0100)

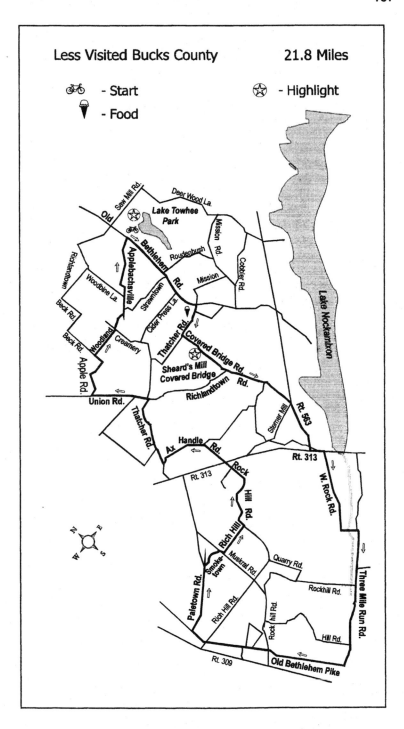

Less Visited Bucks County   21.8 Miles

🚲 - Start   ⭐ - Highlight

🍦 - Food

A majestic tower contributes to the beauty of St. Matthew's Evangelical Lutheran Church.

Nockamixon's East Shore

- 20.5 miles
- Start and end ride at the Three Mile Run Boat Access within Nockamixon Lake State Park
- Terrain: rolling

Highlights

- Nockamixon Lake State Park
- Bucks County farm country
- Elephant Hotel
- St. Matthew's Evangelical Lutheran Church

The area just east of Nockamixon Lake contains some of the most scenic farm country in Bucks County. However, it is still a little to the west of the heavy traffic found in the New Hope-Doylestown corridor. Nockamixon Lake itself is quite lovely and attracts scores of boaters and fishing enthusiasts each year. The 1,450 acre lake is surrounded by Nockamixon State Park, providing outdoor recreation to scores of visitors each year. A swimming pool and snack bar in the park are open from Memorial Day to Labor Day, and boat rentals are available at the lake. There is also a fine multi-use path in the park for walking and bicycling.

At the 1.2 mile mark of the ride, after a short climb, you will see the Elephant Hotel. During the 19th century, the hotel not only housed overnight guests, but served as a political and social center for the surrounding countryside. During prohibition years, it was impossible to maintain the hotel business, so the property became a store. Today, a tavern occupies the first floor of the hotel, which no longer accommodates overnight guests.

A few miles up the road, you cannot help but notice the magnificent architecture of St. Matthew's Evangelical Lutheran Church, built in 1896. The current structure is the fourth church to be built on the site and the congregation is nearly 250 years old.

There are no stores for food purchases along this route. However, you might find the waterfalls, noted at the 5.8 mile mark, to be a pretty place to eat a carry-along picnic. There are also picnic tables and grills at the Three Mile Run Boat Access where the ride begins.

Getting to Three Mile Run Boat Access

Take Route 611 north to the Route 313 exit in Doylestown. Travel west on Route 313 and look for Three Mile Run Road on the right, just past the traffic light at Route 563. It is a small road and easy to miss. A brown and white sign indicating a turn for the "Region Office - State Parks" is another clue to start looking for Three Mile Run Road. Turn right onto Three Mile Run Road from Route 313. The Boat Access is about a mile up the road on the left.

The Ride

0.0	L	From the Three Mile Run Boat Access driveway, make a left turn onto Three Mile Run Road.
0.3	R	Make a right turn at the stop sign onto an unmarked road.
0.4	S	Straight onto Elephant Road.
0.5	BL	Bear left, staying on Elephant Road.(sign says Creek Road West).

1.2	L	Make a left turn onto Ridge Road. The Elephant Hotel is on the right after making the turn.
2.3	BL	Bear left, staying on Ridge Road. Ridge Road becomes South Park Road.
5.8	S	View scenic waterfalls on left!
6.7	R	Make a right turn onto Park Road.
6.8	R	Make a right turn at the Yield sign
7.2	R	Make a right turn onto Creamery Road.
7.6	S	Straight onto Fretz Valley Road.
8.3	L	Make a left turn onto Deer Run Road.
8.9	R	Make a right turn onto Farm School Road.
10.2	R	Make a right turn at the T onto Keller's Church Road (unmarked).
11.6	L	Make a left turn onto Edge Hill Road. Use caution, as oncoming cars will be coming over the crest of a hill.
12.1	L	Make a left turn at the T onto Birch Lane (unmarked).
12.6	R	Make a right turn at the T onto Sweet Briar Road (unmarked).
14.4	L	Make a left turn at the T onto Elephant Road (unmarked).
16.0	R	Make a right turn onto Blue School Road
16.7	R	Make a right turn onto Bucks Road
17.8	R	Make a right turn at the T onto Sweet Briar Road (unmarked).
18.1	L	Make a left turn onto Bucks Road. Begin a steep ascent of a hill.
18.8	L	Make a left turn at the T onto Ridge Road (unmarked).
19.3	R	Make a right turn onto Butler Lane (unmarked).

| 19.9 | R | Make a right turn onto Three Mile Run Road. |
| 20.5 | END | End at the Three Mile Run Boat Access. |

FYI

Nockamixon Lake State Park, Quakertown (215-529-7300)

Bicycle Shops

Bike Line, Main & Old Dublin, Doylestown, PA (215-348-8015)

Cycledrome, 38 South 8th Street, Quakertown, PA (215-536-3443)

Cycle Sports LTD., 641 North Main Street, Doylestown, PA (215-340-2526)

Evolution Pro Bike and Ski Shop, Rts. 413 & 202, Buckingham, PA (215-794-9600)

Freeman's Bicycle Shop, Routes 412 & 563, Ottsville, PA (610-847-5506)

Nestor's Sporting Goods, 99 N. West End Blvd., Quakertown, PA (215-529-0100)

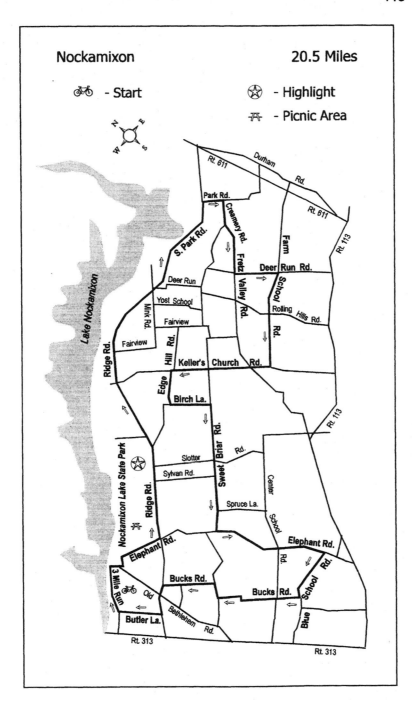

Nockamixon
20.5 Miles

🚲 - Start
⭐ - Highlight
🪑 - Picnic Area

Rocks And Woods: Ringing Rocks Park, Erwinna And Revere

- 25.25 miles
- Start and end at Ringing Rocks Park, just west of Upper Black Eddy
- Terrain: challenging hills

Highlights

- Ringing Rocks Park
- Pretty wooded streams
- Two covered bridges
- Turtle Rock Sutler
- Evermay on-the-Delaware
- Frankenfield Farm Bed & Breakfast

The area between Lake Nockamixon and the Delaware River is sometimes known as the Palisades Region of Bucks County. Traveling in a northeast direction from Lake Nockamixon, the hills get higher and higher before making a very pronounced drop just before the Delaware River. The result is some very challenging yet beautiful country roads for cycling.

The ride begins at Ringing Rocks County Park. The sixty-five acre tract got its name from a boulder field inside the park. Visitors enjoy bringing hammers to the boulder field and listening to the rocks "ring" when tapped. Another fine feature of the park is a small, but beautiful waterfall less than a mile from the boulder field. A hiking trail connects both the boulder field and the waterfall with the parking lot where the ride starts. If time and energy level permit, the short hike is a very nice post-ride activity.

While the ride features many beautiful farms and country homes, much of it travels through thick forests crisscrossed by numerous little streams. Twice on the ride, these streams are crossed by quaint nineteenth century covered bridges that enhance the rural ambiance. The ride passes through the tiny village of Erwinna, named for Colonel Arthur Erwin, a contemporary of George Washington, who owned the surrounding lands in the mid 18th century. Headquarters Road, which leads out of Erwinna, was so named because it contained the offices of the superintendent during the construction of the Delaware Canal.

If you wish to extend your visit, Evermay on-the-Delaware is a very elegant inn at the corner of Geigel Hill and River Roads, two-tenths of a mile from the juncture of Geigel Hill and Headquarters Roads in Erwinna. A two night stay is required on weekends.

Another option is the Frankenfield Farm Bed & Breakfast, owned by Paul and Grace Ringheiser. Built in 1787, the lovely farmhouse features three guest rooms, while a fourth is located in the nearby guest house. Paul told us that it is not uncommon for guests to be able to watch deer crossing the house's back yard. The Frankenfield Farm is located on Frankenfield Road, exactly one mile from the intersection of Frankenfield and Red Hill Roads, along the ride route. At the intersection of Hollow Horn and Red Hill Roads, ride six-tenths of a mile farther along the route to Frankenfield Road. Turn left onto Frankenfield Road and ride one mile uphill. The farm's driveway is clearly marked with a blue and while sign.

Food is available on the ride at The Top of the Mall Deli, reached by continuing on Beaver Run Road at the 20.7 mile point. The deli is located at the intersection of Beaver Run Road with Route 611. There is a picnic area by the parking lot in Ringing Rocks Park.

It should be noted that we experienced a significant amount of loose gravel and potholes on a few of the roads on this ride. However, even on skinny tires, we experienced no real difficulties as long as we rode slowly through the rougher sections. The beauty of the forests and streams makes up for the minor inconveniences.

Getting to Ringing Rocks Park

Ringing Rocks Park is near Upper Black Eddy, located on the Delaware River. From Philadelphia, take Route 95 north to Route 32, and follow Route 32 (River Road) north through New Hope and on up to Upper Black Eddy. Just past the Bridgeton House Bed and Breakfast, turn left onto Bridgeton Hill Road. Go 1.5 miles and turn right onto Ringing Rocks Road.

Alternately, take Route 611 north from Doylestown. Shortly after passing Schoolhouse Apartments, in the tiny town of Revere, Route 611 bears left and you continue straight onto Beaver Run Road. Turn left onto Marienstein Road, continue 3.8 miles, and turn left onto Ringing Rocks Road.

The Ride

0.0	L	From the parking lot at Ringing Rocks County Park, turn left onto Ringing Rocks Road .
0.2	L	Make a left turn at the T onto Bridgeton Hill Road (unmarked).
0.7	R	Make a right turn onto Chestnut Ridge Road (sign for Chestnut Ridge is on the left). The road soon becomes Upper Tinicum Church Road.
3.1	L	Make a left turn onto Union School Road. Caution: loose gravel!
3.2	BR	Bear right onto Upper Tinicum Church Road. (Sign says "Red Cliff Road").

3.6	BR	Bear right, staying on Upper Tinicum Church Road.
3.9	L	Make a left turn at the T onto Perry Auger Road. The road soon becomes Upper Tinicum Church Road again.
5.5	L	Make a left turn onto Geigel Hill Road.
5.8	S	Go through Erwinna Covered Bridge.
6.0	R	Make a right turn onto Headquarters Road (just before the Erwinna Post Office). To get to Evermay on-the-Delaware, continue straight. Turn into the driveway on the right before you get to busy Route 32.
6.9	BR	Bear right onto Tinicum Creek Road.
7.0	L	Make a left turn onto Hollow Horn Road.
8.25	L	Make a left turn at the T, staying on Hollow Horn Road (unmarked).
8.4	S	Turtle Rock Sutler, a whimsical crafts barn owned by Joanne Maschi, is on the left.
8.5	S	Go through the Frankenfield Covered Bridge and continue straight, staying on Hollow Horn Road.
10.6	S	Go straight onto Red Hill Road (Hollow Horn Road turns left).
11.7	R	Turn right onto Headquarters Road.
11.8	R	Turn right, staying on Headquarters Road.
12.35	R	Turn right, staying on Headquarters Road.
14.1	L	Make a left turn onto Cafferty Road. Caution: you will be traveling downhill and the sign is partially obscured by foliage.
15.35	L	Make a left turn onto Geigel Hill/Cafferty Road.
15.45	R	Make a right turn onto Cafferty Road.
16.2	S	Go straight at the stop sign.

16.95	L	Turn left onto Tammany Road. Tammany Road becomes Strocks Grove Road.
18.1	L	Turn left onto Rock Ridge Road.
19.0	R	Turn right onto Byers Road.
19.65	R	Turn right onto Beaver Run Road.
20.7	R	Turn right onto Marienstein Road. (For a short side trip for food, continue .4 mile on Beaver Run Road to the Top of the Mall Deli at the intersection with Route 611. Caution: busy road.)
22.05	R	Turn right onto Lonely Cottage Road.
23.1	BR	Bear right, staying on Lonely Cottage Road.
24.2	BL	Bear left, staying on Lonely Cottage Road.
24.6	S	Go straight at the stop sign.
25.2	R	Turn right onto Ringing Rocks Road.
25.3	END	End ride by turning left into Ringing Rocks County Park.

FYI

Evermay on-the-Delaware, Erwinna (610-294-9100, www.evermay.com)
Frankenfield Farm, Ottsville (610-847-2771)
Ringing Rocks Park, Upper Black Eddy (215-757-0571)
Turtle Rock Sutler, Erwinna (610-294-9394)

Bicycle Shops

Bike Line, 25th Street Shopping Center, Easton, PA (610-253-8103)

Freeman's Bicycle Shop, 52 Bridge Street, Frenchtown, NJ (908-996-7712)

Freeman's Bicycle Shop, Routes 412 & 563, Ottsville, PA (610-847-5506)

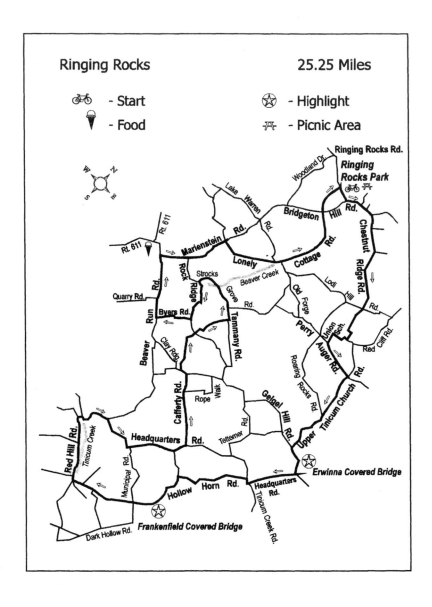

The Foothills of the Poconos:
Lost River Caverns And Durham

- 27.8 miles
- Start and finish at the Hellertown Public Parking Lot
- Terrain: Hilly

Highlights

- Lost River Caverns
- A.L. Bergstresser General Store
- Durham Forge
- Historic Durham Furnace
- Quaint village of Springtown
- Stone Pond Bed & Breakfast

This ride explores the beautiful countryside along the border of Northhampton and Bucks Counties, and contains a few strenuous climbs. However, once you complete the climbs, you are rewarded with beautiful, unobstructed views of the unspoiled pastoral countryside below.

The ride begins at the Hellertown Public Parking Lot, situated on Durham Street between the Dewey Fire Company and the Morris Dimmick Park. In season, you may want to bring a swim suit for a quick dip in the municipal swimming pool, located just across the street. The Morris Dimmick Park contains ball fields, picnic areas and bathrooms. Please note that alcoholic beverages are not allowed in the park.

Almost immediately upon leaving Hellertown, you will see Lost River Caverns on the right. Like Crystal Cave a little farther west, Lost River Caverns afford the visitor the opportunity to go underground and see one of nature's true natural wonders. The first and most challenging climb begins just past the caverns. At the summit, you will find the A.L. Bergstresser General Store. It's worth a stop to browse through its interesting selection of work clothes as well as very basic groceries. Sandwiches cost $1.75 each and the shopkeepers will build them from any combination of meats and cheeses. Seven miles farther up the road is "The Store" in Raubsville, also containing a sandwich selection, but closed on Sundays after 1:00 p.m..

The second climb crosses the ridge that separates Northhampton from Bucks County. Once in Bucks County, your next point of interest is Durham Forge, located, appropriately enough, on Old Furnace Road. Here, Wayne Apgar, who is both the blacksmith and proprietor, will enthusiastically explain his trade, as well as show you samples of his finely crafted candelabras, fireplace sets and garden ornaments. Further ahead is the tiny village of Durham Furnace. The furnace itself no longer stands, but you will find carefully preserved historic homes, as well as a beautifully restored mill.

Finally, before coming back into Hellertown, you will visit the quaint village of Springtown, full of antique stores and a whimsical crafts shop called "Flowers and Crafts by Nancy."

If you would like to take several days to explore this wonderful area, we recommend the Stone Pond Bed & Breakfast. Innkeeper Jerry Hanley prides himself on his hearty breakfasts which include his homemade granola, as well as seasonal produce purchased from local growers and food stands. Each room still has its original pine floor and is decorated with antiques and collectibles to suit its personality. Jerry requires a two-night stay on weekends, while a 25% discount is given during the week. The Inn is located on Route 412, just east of the 20.2 mile mark of the ride (Lehnenberg Road and Route 412). Although the distance between the two points is only half a mile, cyclists starting and ending at the inn should be traffic savvy since this small section of the road has a few sharp curves and is heavily used by motorists later in the day.

Getting to Hellertown

Take the PA Turnpike Northeast Extension north to the Quakertown exit, and then Route 663 north to Route 309 (or else take Route 309 north all the way from Philadelphia). Continue on Route 309 north to Route 378 north. From Route 378, turn right onto Seidersville Road. Continue on this road as it becomes Hickory Hill Road. Turn right on Route 412 in Hellertown (Main Street), go one block and turn left on Penn Street. Penn Street becomes Durham Street. The Hellertown Public Parking Lot and Morris Dimmick Park will be on the right.

The Ride

0.0	R	From the Hellertown Public Parking Lot, make a right turn onto Durham Street.
0.3	S	Pass Lost River Caverns on the right.
0.7	L	Make a left turn onto Wassergass Road. Reservoir Road goes off to the right. Ascend steep hill.
2.5	S	Go straight onto Wassergass Road. The A.L. Bergstressor General Store is on the right.
3.2	BL	Bear left, staying on Wassergass.
3.4	BR	Bear right, staying on Wassergass.
4.0	BL	Bear left, staying on Wassergass.
5.2	S	At the stop sign, go straight onto Raubsville Road. Ahead are beautiful views of the Delaware River Valley. Enjoy a glorious downhill ride into Raubsville.
9.3	R	Make a right turn onto Kiefer Street. A sign will say "To 611." "The Store" is on the left.

9.5	S	Make a quick left onto Young Street and an immediate right back onto Kiefer Street. DO NOT go onto busy Route 611.
9.6	R	Make a right turn onto Mill Street. Ascend a steep hill.
9.9	L	Make a left turn onto Royal Manor Road. Use caution descending winding road. The descent ends with a stop sign on busy 611.
11.1	R	Make a right turn onto Route 611. Fry's Run County Park is on the right, just before the turn.
11.2	R	After crossing a bridge, make a right turn onto Coffeetown Road.
11.4	BL	Bear left, staying on Coffeetown.
12.8	L	Make a left turn onto Durham Road.
13.3	L	Make a left turn onto Stout's Valley Road.
13.8	S	Go straight at the stop sign.
14.3	S	Go straight at the stop sign.
14.8	R	Make a right turn onto Rattlesnake Road.
15.1	BR	Bear right at the stop sign onto Route 212.
15.3	R	Make a right turn onto Old Forge Road. Durham Forge is up the road on the right.
15.8	BL	Bear left. Note the Old Durham Feed Mill on the right. If time permits, the area around the feed mill (now a post office) is worth stopping to visit. The area is also full of beautiful old homes.
16.0	S	Cross Route 212 onto Mine Hill Road.
17.1	R	Make a right turn onto Cross Road.
17.3	R	Make a right turn onto Lehnenberg Road. Cascade Lodge, a beautiful and expensive restaurant, is .2 miles to the left on Lehnenberg Road.
18.6	S	Go straight at the stop sign.
20.2	R	Make a right turn onto Route 412.

20.4	R	Make a right turn onto Bodder Road.
21.1	L	Make a left turn onto Route 212.
23.3	BR	In the village of Springtown, bear right onto Springtown Road. Route 212 bears to the left here. Springtown Road will become Springtown Hill Road, with wonderful views from the top of the hill.
25.6	R	Make a right turn, staying on Springtown Hill Road.
26.0	BR	Bear right, staying on Springtown Hill Road.
26.2	R	Make a right turn onto Route 412.
26.3	R	Make a right turn onto Polk Valley Road.
27.2	L	After going through the Saucon School Complex, make a left turn at the T.
27.3	S	Go straight onto Constitution Ave. Enter Hellertown.
27.7	L	Make a left turn onto Durham Road.
27.8	END	End ride at the Hellertown Public Parking Lot on the left.

FYI

Lost River Caverns, Hellertown (610-838-8767)
Stone Pond Bed and Breakfast, Riegelsville (610-346-6236)

Bicycle Shops

Bike Line, 25th Street Shopping Center, Easton, PA (610-253-8103)

Genesis Bicycles, 126 Bushkill Street, Easton, PA (610-253-1140)

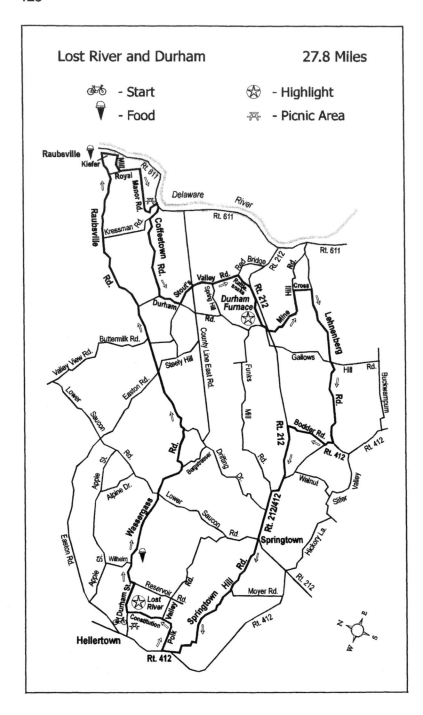

The Peace Valley Ride

- 11.9 miles
- Start and end at the Peace Valley Nature Center
- Terrain: flat to rolling with one steep ascent.

Highlights

- Peace Valley Nature Center
- Peace Valley Park
- Peace Valley Winery
- Tabora Farm & Orchard
- The Pearl S. Buck House
- Stone Ridge Bed and Breakfast

After living halfway around the world, writer Pearl Buck chose the tranquil farmlands of the central Bucks County area for her home. This route gives you the flavor of those farmlands which surround Buck's home. We begin at the Peace Valley Nature Center, a beautiful wildlife preserve located at the northeast end of Lake Galena. Since the ride itself is less than 12 miles, you can spend plenty of time exploring the nature center's 14 mile hiking trail system before or after the tour.

The beginning of the ride makes use of a "bike and hike" path that surrounds most of the lake. Although it is free of motor vehicles, the path may contain numerous pedestrians, especially dog walkers. Therefore slower speeds are the rule and caution is advised. However, the path runs very close to the shoreline and is home to some of the prettiest lakefront riding in the region.

The Peace Valley Winery can be found at the 5.6 mile mark. Two dozen varieties of grapes are grown on 20 acres of land for the winery. A shop and tasting room are located on the premises.

The Pearl Buck House is located at the 8.5 mile mark. Built in 1835, the exterior of the house is a fine example of early rural Pennsylvania architecture. Its interior reflects the famous author's fascination with both Asia and early America. For instance, two Pennsylvania jugs sit on top of the beautifully carved Chinese Hardwood desk at which Buck wrote her famous novel, "The Good Earth."

Food can be purchased seven days a week, all year long at the Tabora Farm and Orchard Store, located at the 5.8 mile mark. Stop in and say hello to Roger Eatherton, who owns the store along with his wife, Jane. "We offer upscale food in a casual country atmosphere," stated Roger on a recent visit, "All the produce is fresh and the food is prepared from scratch. Just this morning the potato salad you see here was potatoes." Roger and Jane have expanded the types of produce and baked goods offered, and in 1999 a catering and a delicatessen section was added on to the store. Gourmet sandwiches and salads are among the many items available here.

The Eathertons own 3000 apple trees and 500 peach trees, in addition to a 4 acre vegetable garden and a one acre flower garden. They enjoy giving back to the community by giving tours of the store and orchard to school children. According to Roger, the children enjoying picking the apples right off the dwarf trees, as well as seeing the cider press in operation.

A Bed and Breakfast called Stone Ridge is located at 956 Bypass Road, 8.8 miles into the ride, and provides a welcome way to enjoy an extended visit to this interesting area.

Getting to the Peace Valley Nature Center

The center is located at 170 Chapman Road. Take Route 611 north to the Route 313 exit in Doylestown. Travel west on Route 313 to New Galena Road (Ginger Bread Square is on the corner).

Make a left turn onto New Galena Road. From New Galena
Road, turn left onto Chapman Road. The parking lot for the nature center will be on the left.

The Ride

0.0	L	From the parking lot at Peace Valley Nature Center (facing the Nature Center buildings), make a left turn onto Chapman Road.
0.2	R	After crossing the bridge, make a right turn onto the bike and hike path.
1.2	S	Go straight. The bike and hike path becomes Creek Road.
1.4	S	Go straight. Cross Old Limekiln Road.
2.15	R	Make a right turn into Peace Valley Park at the Galena Village Entrance (2nd entrance).
2.25	L	Make a left turn onto the bike and hike path, just before the waterfront. Immediately cross a small brown bridge.
3.0	R	Staying on the bike and hike path, make a right turn, crossing the dam to the opposite shore of the lake.
3.4	BR	Bear right, staying on the bike and hike path.
4.65	S	A yellow pole marks the end of the bike and hike path. Continue straight, merging with the driveway (New Galena Road) coming in from the left.
4.8	L	Make a left turn at the T onto Old Limekiln Road (unmarked). A green sign says "winery." Begin ascending a long hill.
5.3	S	Go straight. Cross King Road.
5.6	S	The Peace Valley Winery is on the left.
5.8	L	Make a left turn onto Upper Stump Road.

6.2	R	Make a right turn onto Upper Church Road. Tabora Farm and Orchard Store is on the right, just before the turn.
6.7	R	Make a right turn onto Broad Street.
7.3	L	Make a left turn onto Welcome House Road. The sign is on the left and may be partially obscured by foliage. The road is named after an international adoption agency founded by Pearl S. Buck.
8.2	R	Make a right turn onto Dublin Road.
8.5	S	Go straight. The Pearl Buck House is on the left.
8.6	R	Make a right turn onto Bypass Road (unmarked). It is the first right turn after passing the Pearl Buck House. Stone Ridge Bed and Breakfast will be on the right.
9.2	R	Turn right onto Middle Road.
9.5	S	Go straight. Penn View Farm Store, on the right, has a selection of food and cold drinks.
10.0	L	Turn left onto Upper Stump Road.
10.4	R	Turn right onto Keller Road.
11.0	L	Turn left at the T onto King Road (unmarked).
11.2	R	Turn right onto Chapman Road. Begin a sharp descent into the valley. Caution: stop sign at the bottom of the hill.
11.6.	S	Go straight, crossing New Galena Road. Continue sharp descent.
11.9	END	End the ride at Peace Valley Nature Center.

FYI

Peace Valley Nature Center, New Britain (215-345-7860)
Peace Valley Park, New Britain (215-757-0571)

Peace Valley Winery, Chalfont (215-249-9058)
Pearl S. Buck House, Perkasie (215-249-0100)
Penn View Farm Store, Chalfont (215-249-9128)
Stone Ridge Bed and Breakfast, Perkasie (215-249-3267)
Tabora Farm and Orchard Store, Chalfont (215-249-3016)

Bicycle Shops

Bike Line, Main & Old Dublin, Doylestown, PA (215-348-8015)

Bike Line, Route 202 & 309 & 463, Montgomeryville, PA (215-361-7900)

Cycle Sports LTD., 641 North Main Street, Doylestown, PA (215-340-2526)

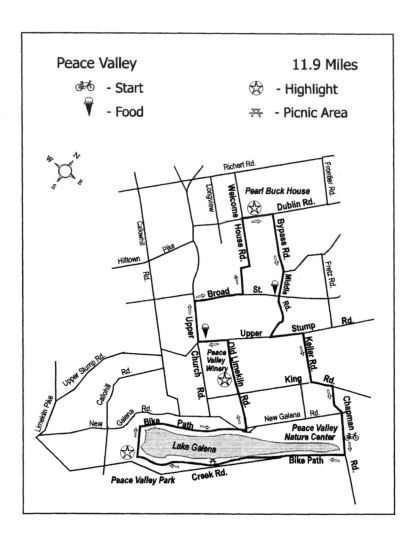

Peace Valley

11.9 Miles

🚲 - Start

✪ - Highlight

🍦 - Food

🪑 - Picnic Area

The Boone Homestead Ramble:
Exeter Township and the Oley Valley

- 47.9 miles
- Start and end at the Daniel Boone Homestead near Birdsboro
- Terrain: Easy rolling hills with two character-building climbs.

Highlights

- Daniel Boone Homestead
- Two splendid downhills
- Reppert's Candy, Inc.
- Two covered bridges
- Oley Turnpike Dairy

"Easy rolling hills," says Barry. But wait a minute, what about those two "character-building" climbs! The first climb, between Lobachsville and Landis Store is nearly three miles long. The second is about a mile long and a little less brutal. Both efforts are rewarded by fast downhills on the other side of the mountain.

The ride begins in Exeter Township, just east of Reading at the site of Daniel's Boone's birth. Since 1938, the property has been owned by the Pennsylvania Historical and Museum Commission, offering a unique glimpse into the lives of the early settlers. In addition to the homestead and other historic structures, the grounds serve as a wildlife refuge where visitors can observe numerous species of animals and birds. The Homestead is open until 5:00 p.m., and the gate across the driveway is closed at that time. If you think there may be a chance that you will not finish the ride before 5:00, you will need to park outside the gate, along side of the driveway or the road.

If the down-hills are not enough incentive to take this ride, the tasty chocolate at Reppert's Candy, Inc. should be. The enterprise, located at the 32.5 mile mark, grew out of a hobby in a building not far from the present site. When Mr. Reppert began to share his delicious candies with his coworkers at Bethlehem Steel, he received the encouragement he needed to begin his business.

Another sweet treat option is the tasty ice cream at the Oley Turnpike Dairy, situated at 37.6 miles. The store sells other farm products typical of the retail dairy outlets in the region, including fresh vegetables in season. At one end of the store is a delicatessen, offering an extensive sandwich menu, as well as soups, salads and bagels.

Food is also available at pizza and sandwich shops in Oley, at the 9 mile point, and at the Pleasantville Inn, near Reppert's Candy at the 32.5 mile point. The Daniel Boone Homestead grounds contain a lovely picnic area as well.

Getting to the Daniel Boone Homestead

The Daniel Boone Homestead is located between Pottstown and Reading, just off of Route 422. From Philadelphia, take either the Pennsylvania Turnpike or the Schuylkill Expressway to King of Prussia and get on Route 422 west. Just before Douglassville, Route 422 is no longer a limited access highway. Begin to look for Daniel Boone Road on the right, just after Limekiln Pike. A prominent brown and white sign points towards the homestead. After turning, continue to follow the signs to the Daniel Boone Homestead. As noted above, if there is any chance that you will not finish the ride by the time the Homestead closes, you need to park outside the gate.

The Ride

0.0	R	From the visitor's center parking lot at the Daniel Boone Homestead, make a right turn and follow the arrows and exit signs out the driveway.
0.5	L	Turn left onto Daniel Boone Road.
1.2	S	Straight, staying on Daniel Boone Road. (On the signpost, both directions say "Daniel Boone Road").
1.9	L	Make a left turn onto Old Tupehocken Road. The sign post is on the left and difficult to see. There is a horse pasture on the right.
2.7	S	Straight, crossing Route 562.
3.5	R	Make a right turn onto Oley Line Road.
4.4	L	Make a left turn onto Limekiln Road.
4.8	L	Make a left turn onto Oley Turnpike.
4.9	R	Make a right turn back onto Limekiln Road.
6.0	R	Make a right turn onto West School Road.
6.5	BL	Bear left, staying on West School Road. (Sign says "Quarry Road").
7.0	BL	Bear left, staying on West School Road.
7.5	R	Make a right turn onto Friedensburg Road.
9.0	S	Cross Route 662, entering the village of Oley. On the left is a small shopping center with a grocery store and a pizza shop. Further up the road is a sandwich shop.
9.2	R	Make a right turn onto Main Street. Enjoy the historic homes and antique stores.
9.6	L	Make a left turn onto Jefferson Street.

11.4	R	Make a right turn onto Mud Run Road (unmarked).
11.5	BR	Bear right, staying on Mud Run Road.
12.0	L	Make a left turn at the stop sign onto Bertolet Mill Road.
12.4	S	Straight, staying on Bertolet Mill Road.
13.9	R	Make a right turn onto Long Lane.
14.6	BL	Make a right turn, staying on Long Lane. (Sign says "Ruppert School Road").
16.6	BL	Bear left, staying on Long Lane.
17.9	R	Make a right turn onto Baldy Hill Road.
17.1	BR	Bear right, staying on Baldy Hill Road.
18.2	S	At the village of Landis Store, Baldy Hill Road becomes Forgedale Road. After Landis Store, there is one more piece of hill climbing before beginning the descent to Barto!
23.7	R	Make a right turn onto Old Route 100.
25.2	R	Make a right turn onto Oberholzer Road.
25.5	R	Make a right turn onto Hill Church Road.
25.7	BL	Bear left, staying on Hill Church Road.
28.1	L	Make a left turn at the stop sign and a quick right back onto Hill Church Road.
30.9	L	Make a left turn onto Oysterdale Road. Caution: this looks like an intersection with a four-way stop, but traffic to your left does not have a stop sign.
32.5	S	Straight, crossing Route 73 at Pleasantville. Ignore signs stating that the bridge is out and there is no outlet. Reppert's Candy, Inc. is to the right on Route 73, and the Pleasantville Inn is on the left.

32.9	L	Just before the covered bridge (closed to traffic), make a left turn onto Toll House Road.
33.8	R	Make a right turn onto Manatawny Road.
34.8	R	Make a right turn onto Spangsville Road. Graber Lettering is on the left.
35.1	S	Go through the covered bridge. Stay well to the right after the bridge, allowing oncoming traffic to make the curve.
35.4	R	Make a right turn onto Church Road.
35.6	L	Make a left turn at the T onto Covered Bridge Road (unmarked).
36.4	R	Make a right turn onto the Oley Turnpike.
37.3	S	Go straight, staying on the Oley Turnpike.
37.6	S	Pass the Oley Turnpike Dairy on the right.
38.8	R	Make a right turn onto Bieber Mill Road (unmarked). Look for a sign saying "Oley Quarry, Crushed Limestone."
39.8	L	At the intersection with Quarry Road, make a left turn, staying on Bieber Mill Road. The sign is on the left and hard to see. It is at the bottom of a short gentle hill.
41.1	L	Make a left turn at the T onto West School Road (unmarked).
41.3	L	Make a left turn onto Limekiln Road.
42.4	L	Make a left turn at the T onto Oley Turnpike (unmarked).
42.5	R	Make a right turn back onto Limekiln Road.
42.9	R	Make a right turn onto Oley Line Road.
43.8	BL	At the intersection with Luder Road, bear left, staying on Oley Line Road.

44.6	S	Continue straight. Oley Line Road becomes Old Tupehocken Road.
45.4	R	Make a right turn onto Daniel Boone Road
46.8	R	Make a right turn into the Daniel Boone Homestead.
47.9	END	End at the Visitor's Center.

FYI

Daniel Boone Homestead, Birdsboro (610-582-4900)
Oley Turnpike Dairy, Oley (610-689-9366)
Reppert's Candy, Pleasantville (610-689-9200)

Bicycle Shops

Bike Line, 1386 N. State Street, Pottstown, PA (610-326-0780)

Lebo's Pedal Parlor, 2200 Penn Ave., West Lawn, PA (610-678-3191)

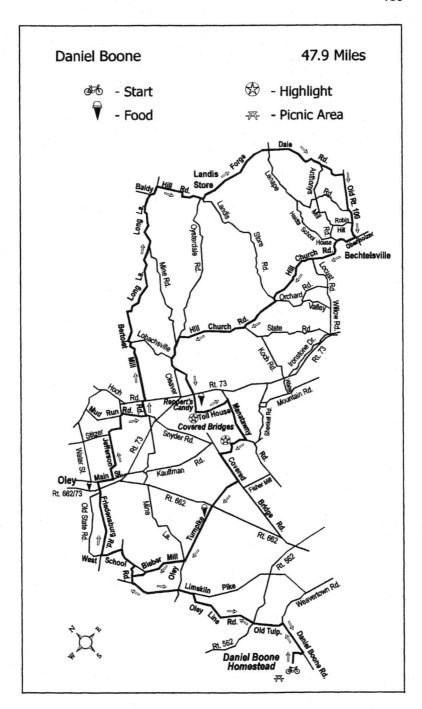

America In Miniature:
Roadside America And Shartlesville

- 20.8 miles
- Start and end at Roadside America, Shartlesville
- Terrain: rolling

Highlights

- Roadside America
- Antiques and crafts stores
- Haag's Hotel
- Beautiful Irish Creek

Founded in 1765, Shartlesville is located on the northern edge of Berks County's farmlands. Just a little outside the center of the village is Roadside America, a truly exciting exhibit for the whole family. "Be Prepared to See More Than You Expect" reads a sign on the front of the building. With 300 beautifully crafted miniature buildings and 2,250 feet of train and trolley tracks, Roadside America attracts visitors from all over the world.

If model trains and miniature buildings attract people to Roadside America, antiques and Pennsylvania Dutch cooking attract people to Shartlesville itself. Famous for the latter is Haag's Hotel. The Haag/Seitzinger family has been serving Pennsylvania Dutch foods for five generations, occupying the current building since 1915. The hotel's specialty is all you can eat, family-style dinners, using traditional Pennsylvania Dutch recipes and including fifteen or more side dishes! In season, all fresh fruits and vegetables are brought into the hotel from adjoining neighborhood farms. Dairy products, as well as the tasty apple butter, are also locally produced. If you cannot stay in the area for dinner, you may want to try one of the hotel's delicious and inexpensive breakfasts or lunches.

Getting to Shartlesville

From the Philadelphia area, take Route 422 west to Reading. In Reading, take Route 222 north to Route 183 north. Just beyond the village of Bernville, make a right turn onto Shartlesville Road and follow it to Shartlesville. Once inside the town, make a left turn onto Olde Route 22 to get to Roadside America.

The Ride

0.0	R	Begin the ride in the parking lot in front of Roadside America. Turn right into the driveway between Roadside America and the Pennsylvania Dutch Gift Haus (just before the statue of the Amish people).
0.1	L	Make a left turn onto Olde 22.
1.2	R	After traveling through downtown Shartlesville, make a right turn onto Schoolhouse Road.
2.7	L	Make a left turn at the stop sign onto Skyline Drive.
3.3	S	Go straight at the yield sign, staying on Skyline Drive.
4.4	S	Go straight. Skyline Drive becomes Lesher's Mill Road.
5.3	L	Make a left turn at the T onto Tilden Road.
5.7	S	Go straight at the stop sign, staying on Tilden Road.

6.7	R	Make a right turn onto Berne Road.
8.1	R	Make a right turn, staying on Berne Road. The sign on the left says "North End Road."
8.4	S	Go straight at the stop sign, entering the village of Centerport.
8.6	R	Turn right onto Irish Creek Road.
10.4	BR	Bear right, staying on Irish Creek Road.
13.4	BR	Bear right at the yield sign, staying on Irish Creek Road.
15.4	R	Turn right onto Shartlesville Road.
16.0	L	Turn left onto Manbeck Road. Use caution when making this turn.
17.9	S	Go straight at the stop sign, staying on Manbeck Road.
18.8	R	Make a right turn onto Spring Road. Spring Road becomes Tulpehocken Road.
20.0	R	Make a right turn onto Olde 22.
20.7	L	Make a left turn into Roadside America.
20.8	END	End the ride in front of Roadside America.

FYI

Haag's Hotel, Shartlesville (610-488-6692)
Roadside America, Shartlesville (610-488-6241)

Bicycle Shop

Spokes Bike Shop, Route 61, Hamburg, PA (610-562-8900)

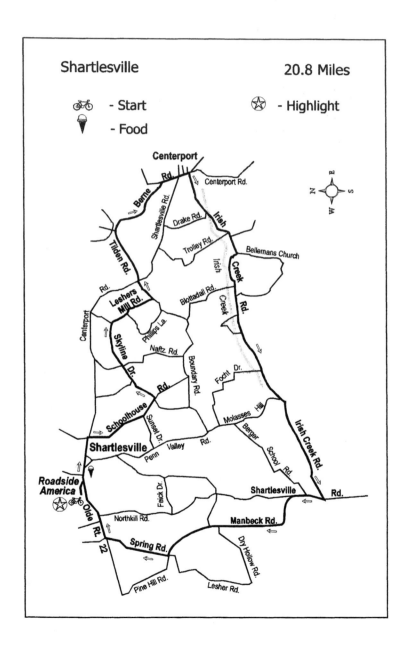

Shartlesville

20.8 Miles

🚲 - Start ⊛ - Highlight

🍦 - Food

Geology And Dutch Food: Crystal Cave, Maiden Creek And Kutztown

- 22.8 miles (26.2 miles with optional side trip to Kutztown)
- Start and end at Crystal Cave
- Terrain: hilly

Highlights

- Crystal Cave
- Two covered bridges
- Maiden Creek
- Pennsylvania Dutch food
- Kutztown Pennsylvania-German Festival (June 26th through July 4)
- Crystal Bed and Breakfast

There is so much to do in this part of Pennsylvania that it is tempting to skip the ride and just visit the attractions. But it is best to get at least a little exercise before hitting those Pennsylvania Dutch restaurants!

The ride begins at the famous Crystal Cave, the oldest operating cave in Pennsylvania. Breath-taking stalagmite and stalactite formations make the cave worth visiting after the ride. Time permitting, we also recommend the side trip to Kutztown. The village is home to a fine university and a world-class fairground. If you did not already sample the Dutch-style food in Lenhartsville, Kutztown has a lively downtown area with many possibilities for lunch and shopping. From June 26th through July 4th annually, the fairgrounds hosts the Kutztown German-American Folk Festival, featuring 200 of America's finest folk artists and craftsmen.

Options for an overnight stay range are numerous and varied. Right along the bicycle route is the Crystal Bed & Breakfast. An 1850's summer kitchen has been converted into a cozy cottage. Designed for only one set of guests at a time, the accommodations consist of a downstairs efficiency kitchen and an upstairs sleeping area with a queen sized bed and private deck. Owners Bob and Nancy Hippert promise their guests the opportunity to step back into a world of clear air and simple pleasures.

You may want to consider walking your bike through the Dreibelbis Covered Bridge, especially if you are riding on very narrow racing tires. Barry is an experienced "plank rider" and still nearly took a spill on the this bridge.

Getting To Crystal Cave

From the greater Philadelphia area, take Route 422 to Reading. At Reading, take Route 222 north to Route 662 North at Moselem Springs. After about a mile, bear right onto Route 143 and travel a little over two miles to Virginville. From Virginville, bear right on Crystal Cave Road and follow the signposts for Crystal Cave.

The Ride

0.0	L	From the entrance to Crystal Cave (Valley Road) make a left turn onto Crystal Cave Road.
1.5	S	Pass Crystal Cave Bed & Breakfast on the left, continuing straight on Crystal Cave Road.
2.6	R	Make a sharp right onto Dunkel's Church Road. (If you get to Route 143, you went too far!)
3.8	R	Make a right turn onto Sunday Road. Look for a pretty pale yellow house at the top of the hill..

4.6	L	Make a left turn onto Hummel's Hill Road.
4.9	R	Make a right turn onto Dunkel's Church Road. Caution: you go abruptly into a short steep climb.
5.6	L	Make a left turn onto Miller Road (at dairy farm).
6.7	R	Make a right turn onto Dreibelbis Station Road.
7.0	L	Make a left turn onto Covered Bridge Road. Pass through the Dreibelbis Station Covered Bridge. Caution: wooden planks inside bridge!
7.1	R	Right onto Route 143. View beautiful Maiden Creek on your left.
8.7	L	Make a left turn, staying on Route 143 North. Enter the village of Lenhartsville.
8.9	R	Make a right turn, staying on Route 143. The Deitsch Eck restaurant is on this corner and worth making a stop if you are hungry. After making the turn, you will also see J. Hummel's Restaurant.
11.8	R	Make a right turn onto Little Round Top Road.
11.9	R	Make a right turn, staying on Little Round Top Road. Begin a short, but serious climb!
14.1	L	Make a left turn onto Old Route 22.
14.4	R	Make a right turn onto Kohler's Hill Road (look for sign that says "Kutztown 6").
17.3	S	Go straight and merge onto Route 737. Caution: busy road!
18.4	R	Make a right turn onto Kutz Mill Road (Look for sign saying "Archery Shop").
19.0	S	Pass through Kutz Mill Covered Bridge.
19.4	R	Make a right turn onto Saucony Road.
		Optional side trip to Kutztown: To get to Kutztown, make a left turn onto Kutztown

College Boulevard at this intersection. Bear right at the one mile mark. The fairgrounds and the university will be another .7 miles down the road. The village proper is just a little beyond the university. To rejoin the ride, simply turn around and go back to the intersection of College Boulevard, Kutz Mill and Saucony Roads. Go straight onto Saucony Road.

20.1	BL	At Dutch Mill Campsites, bear left, staying on Saucony Road.
22.5	L	Make a left turn onto Crystal Cave Road.
22.8	END	End ride at entrance to Crystal Cave (also called Valley Road).

FYI

Crystal Cave, Kutztown (610-683-6765)
Crystal Bed & Breakfast, Kutztown (610-683-7081)
Deitsch Eck Restaurant, Lenhartsville (610-562-8520)
Kutztown Pennsylvania German Festival, Kutztown (888-674-6136)

Bicycle Shops

Bicycle Den, 226 West Main Street, Kutztown, PA (610-683-5566)

Spokes Bike Shop, Route 61, Hamburg, PA (610-562-8900)

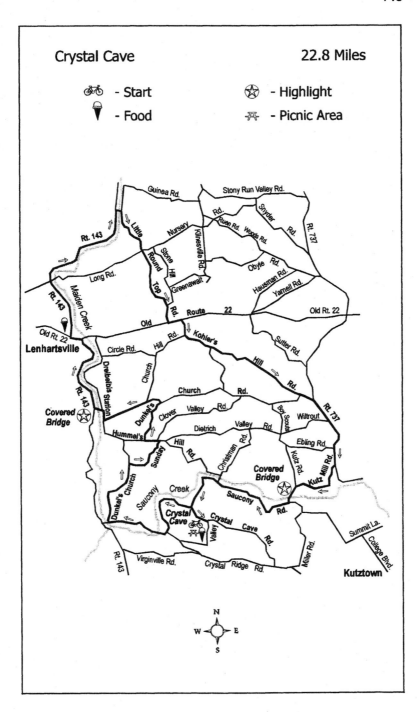

Crystal Cave

22.8 Miles

🚲 - Start

⭐ - Highlight

🍦 - Food

🪧 - Picnic Area

Rails And Sails:
Leaser Lake and Kempton

- 31.3 miles (36.5 miles with optional side trip to Hawk
  Mountain or 32.2 miles with optional side trip to Leaser
  Lake)
- Start and finish at the W.K.& S. Steam Railroad in Kempton
- Terrain: rolling with a few steep climbs

Highlights

- W.K.& S. Steam Railroad
- Hawk Mountain
- Leaser Lake
- Mountain scenery
- Gloria's Forget-Me-Not Bed and Breakfast

This route provides an excellent opportunity to explore the
beautiful farmlands along the base of the rugged Blue Mountain.
The region is probably most famous for the wildlife sanctuary,
created by environmentalists in the 1930s, on top of Hawk
Mountain. The unique air currents make Hawk Mountain's rocky
lookout one of the most ideal spots in North America to view the
annual hawk migrations. During the height of the autumn season,
visitors come for all over the world to enjoy the hawks, as well as
the spectacular scenery.

The main route of the ride is mostly rolling hills with only a
few short steep climbs. However, the optional side trip up Hawk
Mountain is the most difficult climb in this book, if not the most

difficult climb in southeastern Pennsylvania! In 1989, the climb also gained the attention of cycling enthusiasts when it was included as part of a stage in the inaugural Tour de Trump.

A much less ambitious undertaking is the optional side trip to Leaser Lake. The lake is small as bodies of water go, although large enough for sailing and fishing, and is a very pretty place to enjoy a break and perhaps a picnic lunch.

Another attraction of interest is the W.K. & S. Steam Railroad, located at the starting point. During the summer, rail fans can enjoy an old fashioned train ride alongside Ontelaunee Creek. The railroad is also open during the autumn, but only on weekends.

There is one restaurant along the route. At the 17 mile mark, you will find the Hotel New Tripoli prominently located in the center of the town of the same name. Complete meals, in addition to sandwiches, are served in a lively tavern atmosphere, Monday through Saturday. At 11.85 miles, the village of Wanamakers contains a general store with a very nice selection of dried fruits, nut mixes and homemade baked goods. The Kempton Hotel, located near the start and open Wednesday through Monday, is another option for a meal before or after the ride.

Gloria's Forget-Me-Not Bed and Breakfast is located on Hawk Mountain Road at the 1.1 mile mark on the ride, and offers accommodations in either the beautiful guest house or in a private cottage with a jacuzzi tub. Gloria's full breakfast, possibly featuring blueberry pancakes and Texas bacon, is a fine start to your day in this wonderfully scenic area.

Getting to Kempton

From the Philadelphia area, take either Route 309 north or the northeast extension of the PA turnpike to Route 78 west. At the Lenhartsville exit take Route 143 north. Turn right onto Route 737 and follow the road into Kempton. Turn onto Creek Road just past the Kempton Hotel, following the signs for the W.K.& S. Railroad.

The Ride

0.0	S	From the parking lot of the W.K. & S. Railroad, with the trains on your right, go straight out the Community Center Drive.
0.1	S	Straight at the stop sign.
0.15	R	Make a right turn at the second stop sign. The sign says "Kistler Valley Road."
0.25	R	Make a right turn onto Route 737.
0.7	L	Make a left turn onto Route 143.
1.1	R	Make a right turn onto Hawk Mountain Road. Look for sign saying "Hawk Mountain Bird Sanctuary." Gloria's Forget-Me-Not Bed & Breakfast is the second house on the right after making the turn. A prominent rock outcropping called the Pinnacle can be viewed on the left while traveling this road.
5.2	R	Make a right turn onto Mountain Road. **Optional side trip to Hawk Mountain Sanctuary:** To get to the Hawk Mountain Sanctuary, continue on Hawk Mountain Road instead of making this turn. Follow Hawk Mountain Road 2.6 miles to the sanctuary. This road could be busy during the autumn season. To rejoin the ride, simply turn around and ride back to the intersection of Hawk Mountain Road and Mountain road. (Be very careful descending the mountain). Turn left onto Mountain Road.
8.5	L	Make a left turn onto Quaker City Road. The sign is on the left and easy to miss.
9.9	S	Continue straight. Quaker City Road becomes Slateville Road.

10.9		**Optional side trip to Leaser Lake:** To get to Leaser Lake, turn left here onto Utt Road. Continue for .5 mile and turn left onto Leaser Road. In .1 mile, turn right at the sign pointing to Leaser Lake and ride .3 mile farther to the lake. To return to the bike ride, retrace your way back to Slateville Road and turn left.
11.3	L	Make a left turn onto Route 143. Watch for Wanamakers General Store.
11.9	R	Make a right turn onto Allemaengel Road.
12.4	S	Continue straight, staying on Allemaengel Road.
13.2	BL	Bear left, staying on Allemaengel Road.
13.7	BL	Bear left, staying on Allemaengel Road.
14.0	R	Turn right, staying on Allemaengel Road.
16.6	S	Straight at stop sign in New Tripoli onto Decator Street.
17.0	S	Continue straight. The Hotel New Tripoli is the large yellow building on your extreme right.
17.2	R	Make a right turn onto Washington Street, at the end of town.
17.3	S	Go straight at the stop sign. Washington Street becomes Camp Meeting Road.
18.4	L	Make a left turn onto Flint Hill Road.
20.7	R	Make a right turn onto Werley's Corner Road.
23.5	R	Make a right turn onto Holben's Valley Road.
25.5	S	Go straight. Holben's Valley Road becomes Kistler Valley Road.
31.1	R	Make a right turn onto Creek Road.
31.2	BR	Bear right onto Community Drive.
31.3	END	End ride at W.K & S. Railroad.

FYI

Gloria's Forget-Me-Not Bed and Breakfast, Kempton (610-756-3398)
Hawk Mountain, Kempton (610-756-6961)
Kempton Hotel, Kempton (610-756-6588)
W.K. & S. Railroad, Kempton (610-756-6469)
Wanamakers General Store, Wanamakers (610-756-6558)

Bicycle Shops

Bicycle Den, 226 West Main Street, Kutztown, PA (610-683-5566)

Bike Line, 1728 Tilghman Street, Allentown, PA (610-439-1724)

Bike Line, 831 Chestnut Street, Emmaus, PA (610-967-1029)

Spokes Bike Shop, Route 61, Hamburg, PA (610-562-8900)

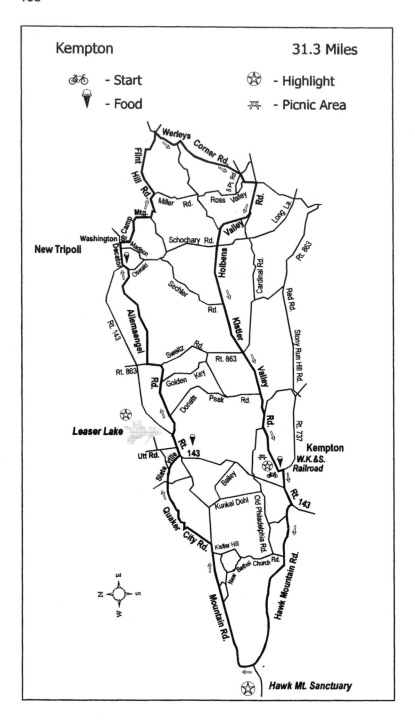

Kempton

31.3 Miles

🚲 - Start

🍦 - Food

✪ - Highlight

🪑 - Picnic Area

Following The Tire Tracks of LeMond: Orwigsburg and Hawk Mountain

- 17.5 miles
- Start and finish at the Orwigsburg Community Parking Center
- Terrain: rolling

Highlights

- Historic Orwigsburg
- Pennsylvania Dutch countryside
- Views of renowned Hawk Mountain
- Serenity Farm Milkhouse

Twice the southern portion of Schuylkill County played host to the world's greatest cyclists, including Greg LeMond. At one point in its colorful history, the area also hosted "The Greatest." In the early 1970s, heavyweight champ Muhammad Ali built a training facility just across Route 61 from Deer Lake.

The ride begins in Orwigsburg, a one-time town of the Tour Du Pont and now home to many antique and craft shops. The route quickly moves into some very rural country. Many of the roads are unnamed on local maps and unmarked along the ride, and a bicycle computer is practically a necessity in order to follow the route. At numerous points throughout the ride, outstanding views of famous Hawk Mountain are afforded. During the first quarter of this century, Hawk Mountain was a popular place to hunt birds of prey. However, for over fifty years, the summit of the mountain has been preserved as a sanctuary, attracting visitors from all over the world.

Food is available in Orwigsburg at a number of pizza and sandwich shops. Recently reopened is the Inn at Orwigsburg, conveniently located on the square. You can also purchase tasty ice cream and hot dogs at Maple Leaf Farm, located at the 6.2 mile mark along the route.

You can combine cycling with hiking on the Appalachian Trail or antique shopping in Orwigsburg to fill a whole weekend. Right along the route is Serenity Farm, featuring a "milk house" that was converted into a single unit lodging facility overlooking the farm's pond. Owners Felix and Sherry Bartush renovated the structure to create a unique living and dining area, a modern kitchen and a second story sleeping loft. Felix and Sherry have also converted part of their farmhouse into a country inn. Serenity Farm and Milk House is located on Red Dale Road, 1.8 miles east of Orwigsburg.

Getting to Orwigsburg

From the Philadelphia area, take Route 422 to Reading. In Reading, leave Route 422 to enter Route 61 north. Just past the village of Deer Lake, look for a sign to the right pointing to Orwigsburg. Follow that road into town. Once in town, the road becomes Market Street. In the center of town is a very pretty square. The community parking lot is located on the right side of the square at Warren Street.

The Ride

| 0.0 | R | From the Orwigsburg Community Parking Center (at the corner of Market and Warren Streets), make a right turn onto Market Street. Enjoy a long downhill through the center of town. |

0.4	R	At the Orwigsburg Post Office, make a right turn onto Lincoln Avenue.
1.0	R	Make a right turn onto Second Mountain Road (unmarked). A sign says "Ruff's Nursery."
2.55	BL	Bear left and enjoy a nice gradual downhill.
3.8	R	After passing the Swiss Chalet Restaurant, make a right turn at the T onto Pine Creek Drive (unmarked).
4.2	S	Go straight, crossing Route 443.
4.6	L	Make a left turn onto Whitetail Lane (unmarked). Pass a green house on the right after making the turn.
4.95	R	Make a right turn onto Frisbee Road. Descend a half-mile hill. Watch the curves!
5.6	R	Make a right turn onto Red Dale Road (unmarked). A red garage is on the right.
5.9	L	Make a left turn onto Pine Creek Road (unmarked). Watch for a sign for Maple Leaf Farm.
6.2	S	Maple Leaf Farm is on the right.
6.25	L	Make a left turn at the T, staying on Pine Creek Road. A white church is on the right just before the turn. Local cyclists have reported to us that they have observed cars running the stop sign. Please use caution!
7.3	L	Make a left turn onto Pheasant Run Road.
7.6	R	Make a right turn onto Lake Front Drive (unmarked).
8.4	R	Make a right turn at the stop sign, staying on Lake Front Drive (unmarked).
8.8	S	Straight on Lake Front Drive.
9.0	L	After viewing the lake on the right, make a left turn onto Spruce Road.

9.35	R	Make a right at the T onto Coal Mountain Road (unmarked). Begin ascending a hill.
9.95	L	Make a left turn at the intersection at the top of the hill (unmarked). A sign ahead says "Pavement Ends, 550 feet." Enjoy a mile long downhill, but watch the curves!
11.1	L	At the bottom of the hill, make a left turn at the T onto Stephens Drive (unmarked).
11.85	R	Make a right turn onto Pheasant Run Road (unmarked) at the four way stop sign. There are good views of Hawk Mountain on the right.
12.6	L	Make a left turn at the T onto Rabbit Run Road.
12.8	L	Make a left turn onto Red Dale Road (unmarked).
16.75	BL	Bear left. Red Dale Road becomes Lawrence Street.
17.0	R	Make a right turn onto Mifflin Street.
17.4	L	Make a left turn onto Warren Street.
17.5	END	End the ride at Warren and Market Streets.

FYI

Serenity Farm and Milk House, Orwigsburg (570-943-2919)
The Inn at Orwigsburg, Orwigsburg (570-366-3658)

Bicycle Shops

Spokes Bike Shop, Route 61, Hamburg, PA (610-562-8900)

Weller's Bicycles, 1590 West Market Street, Pottsville, PA (570-622-2743)

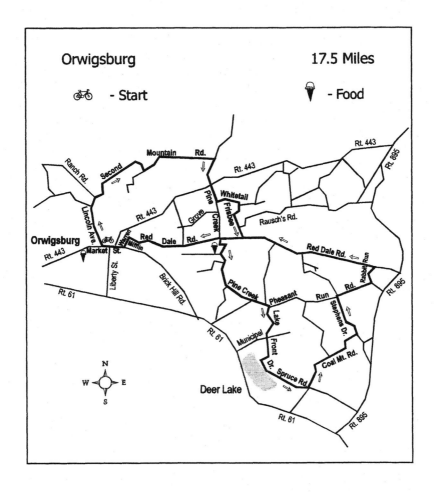

Orwigsburg   17.5 Miles

🚲 - Start   🍦 - Food